Warrior • 104

Tudor Knight

Christopher Gravett • Illustrated by Graham Turner

First published in Great Britain in 2006 by Osprey Publishing,
Midland House, West Way, Botley, Oxford OX2 0PH, UK
44-02 23rd St, Suite 219, Long Island City, NY 11101, USA
Email: info@ospreypublishing.com

Transferred to digital print on demand 2010

First published 2006
1st impression 2006

Printed and bound by Cadmus Communications, USA

A CIP catalogue record for this book is available from the British Library

ISBN: 978 1 84176 970 7

Page layout by Ken Vail Graphic Design
Index by Alison Worthington
Originated by United Graphics, Singapore

Dedication
As always, for Jane and Joanna.

Author's acknowledgement
I should like to thank His Grace the Duke of Bedford and the Trustees of the Bedford Estates for permission to recreate the colour
plate of John Russell. My thanks also to Tobias Capwell at the Kelvingrove Museum in Glasgow for his help and advice concerning
the armour of the Earl of Pembroke. Philip Lankester at the Royal Armouries kindly provided useful information on edged weapons,
while Philip Abbott sought out numerous images.

Artist's note
Readers may care to note that the original paintings from which the colour plates in this book were prepared are available for
private sale. All reproduction copyright whatsoever is retained by the Publisher. Enquiries should be addressed to:

Graham Turner
PO Box 568
Aylesbury
HP17 8ZX
UK
www.studio88.co.uk

The Publishers regret that they can enter into no correspondence upon this matter.

The Woodland Trust
Osprey Publishing is supporting the Woodland Trust, the UK's leading woodland conservation charity, by funding the
dedication of trees.

www.ospreypublishing.com

CONTENTS

TUDOR KNIGHT

INTRODUCTION

Knighthood in the Tudor period had come a long way since 1066. Increasingly, knights could be made from gentlemen who did not have a knightly background, while other eligible candidates were content to remain squires – men of standing, yet happy to forego the expense and the burdens of sitting in parliament or attending law courts. Those who fought often did so as officers in an increasingly professional army.

The Tudor period in England began with a new dynasty in a Catholic land after years of struggle, and would end with a Protestant country whose monarch had ruled for nearly 50 years. The battle of Bosworth in 1485 effectively ended the Wars of the Roses and ushered in the Tudor dynasty. Henry VII, whose father was the Welsh nobleman Edmund Tudor, became king of a country sick of war and uncertainty. Having removed all potential threats, his reign became one of parsimonious husbandry so that, on his death in 1509, he left a prosperous throne to his son and namesake. The earlier legacy of political unrest enabled Henry VIII to wreak his will on a country that allowed him to get away with much providing he held it securely. Despite this, Henry was always wary of potential revolt. Three times he invaded France and made various truces, including that with Francis at the spectacular Field of Cloth of Gold in 1520. However, his vain attempts to play the giant in Europe with fellow rulers Francis I of France and the Emperors Maximilian I and Charles V of Germany ultimately proved futile. Henry kept the Scots in check but his greatest legacy was breaking England away from the Catholic Church in order to divorce his first wife, Catherine of Aragon. There followed the destruction of religious houses across England, their wealth stolen and precious objects melted down. The Pilgrimage of Grace, a rising of northern folk in 1536–37 against corrupt officials, was crushed ruthlessly. By the end of Henry VIII's reign his finances were in a parlous state.

When Henry died in 1547 his sickly son, Edward VI, took the throne at nine years old, surrounded by powerful advisors. When Edward died in 1553 Lady Jane Grey, granddaughter of Henry VIII's younger sister, was put forward as Queen, but executed in 1554. Edward's sister, Mary I, took the throne and reintroduced Catholicism by fire and sword, even sending her youngest sister, Princess Elizabeth, to the Tower of London.

BELOW **Brass of Sir Humphrey Stanley in Westminster Abbey, 1505. His tassets are still strapped on in the earlier English fashion, a little way up the fauld rather than from its lower edge.**

Mary married the Catholic Philip of Spain in a move guaranteed to alienate many Englishmen. When she died in 1558 Elizabeth took over the throne.

Elizabeth I brought back Protestantism and saw off the threat from Mary, Queen of Scots, granddaughter of Henry's sister, Margaret, having her beheaded in 1587. Elizabeth faced the Spanish Armada in 1588, which was chased up the Channel before dashing itself to pieces in the stormy waters around the northern and western coasts of Britain. She toyed with important suitors but never married and so left no heir when she died in 1603. Now the son of Mary, Queen of Scots, James VI of Scotland, took the throne as James I of the House of Stuart.

CHRONOLOGY

1485 Battle of Bosworth and death of Richard III. Accession of Henry VII (House of Tudor)
1509 Death of Henry VII. Accession of Henry VIII
1511 English archers sent to Low Countries to assist Margaret of Savoy against duke of Guelders
1511–12 English forces sent to Spain to assist Ferdinand of Aragon
1513 First invasion of France and siege of Thérouanne
Battle of the Spurs
Battle of Flodden Field
1520 Field of Cloth of Gold
1522 Second invasion of France
1523 Capture of Bray, Roye and Mondidier
Fourth invasion of France
1536–37 Pilgrimage of Grace
1541 Henry VIII proclaimed King of Ireland
1542 Capture of English raiders in Scotland at Haddon Rig
Battle of Solway Moss
1543–44 Third invasion of France
1544 Siege of Montreil
Siege of Boulogne
1545 Scots defeat English at Ancrum Moor
1546 Surrey defeated outside Boulogne
1547 Death of Henry VIII. Accession of Edward VI
Battle of Pinkie
1549 Uprisings in southern England
Kett's Rebellion defeated at Dussindale
1553 Death of Edward VI. Accession of Mary I
1554 Execution of Lady Jane Grey
1557 Battle of St Quentin. Spanish victory over the French. English troops under Pembroke assist in siege of the city that followed
1558 Death of Mary I. Accession of Elizabeth I
1559 Campaign to Normandy
1560 Expedition to Scotland
1561 Attacks by O'Neills of Tyrone defeated
1567 Uprising of Shane O'Neill ends with his death
Abdication of Mary, Queen of Scots
1569–70 Northern Rebellions
1569–73 First Desmond War in Ireland
1572 300 volunteers cross to the Low Countries
1575 Revolt by Fitzgeralds of Ireland
1579–83 Second Desmond War in Ireland

ABOVE **Brass of John Le Strange at Hillingdon, Middlesex, 1509. Small tassets hang round the fauld.**

5

ORGANISATION

Henry VIII

There was no standing army in England for much of the 16th century. Whatever the advantages a standing army may have offered, the monarchs still recalled the nobility backed by their private retinues in times of war. How much more effective and dangerous could they be, then, if they commanded a standing army that was even better trained? Standing armies were, moreover, more expensive and had to be fed even when inactive during the winter. Generally speaking, the lack of troops ready for immediate action did not cause too great a problem and invasions could be planned well ahead of schedule, with enough time to raise the required forces.

BELOW **Henry VIII meets Maximilian I during the siege of Thérouanne in 1513. The German horsemen (on the left) mainly wear sallets, whilst the English cavalry have armets; all wear cloth bases. Their lances are tipped with coronel points as though for jousting, possibly a symbol of peaceful negotiation. The battle of the Spurs is depicted in the background. (The Royal Collection © 2005 Her Majesty Queen Elizabeth II)**

The only bodies that might be regarded as a standing force were small. Two were royal guards; the 'King's Spears', active between 1510 and 1515, comprised men of noble or gentle birth formed together as a royal bodyguard. There were 50 men in all, each supported by a light cavalryman, an archer and a mounted attendant. In 1539 a similar body called the 'Gentlemen Pensioners' was set up (surviving as the Corps of Gentlemen-at-Arms). Of lesser rank were the Yeomen of the Guard created by Henry VII. Fortresses and castles maintained garrisons but although some were large, such as at the touch point of Berwick, others only held a handful of men. In all, this force of 2,000–3,000 men was widely scattered and not generally useful for repressing unrest or providing troops for foreign adventures.

During the early years of the 16th century the magnates still came to the muster with their retainers as they had in the 15th century, being contracted or indentured for a set period (the indenture was a contract cut along a wavy or 'indented' line to provide a portion for the retained man). Henry VIII appears to have given up the contract itself but gentlemen and nobility still brought retinues for foreign expeditions. These retinues varied in size from a few hundred to well over 800, their numbers depending upon the amount of property held – Sir Henry Willoughby was contracted to supply 830 men for the Guienne expedition in 1512. The retinue was usually made up of varying numbers of men-at-arms, archers, handgunners, billmen, halberdiers and pikemen. Tenants might perhaps send substitutes but landowners, if not ill or too young, might have to serve as captains even if already in government positions. Those tenants from royal manors or religious estates were attached to the steward, who might be an aristocrat.

By the time of the 1513 invasion of France some retinues were being divided up into companies 100 or so strong, led by a captain; this was seemingly an attempt to provide more orderly groups at least on the march, though groups of men below 100 – such as the 66 brought by Thomas Lucy – were not joined with others to make up the numbers. For the 1522 invasion far more units consisted of companies of 100 men under a captain (at four shillings a day) and a petty-captain. By mid-century this was the accepted format, the above officers being joined by a standard-bearer, sergeant and four vinteners (corporals) each responsible for 25 of the men (privates). Thomas Audley in his *A.B.C. for the Wars* (written for the boy Edward VI but harking back to experiences under Henry VIII) remarks that 200 is a better number for a captain, since then he would receive eight shillings and be less likely to palm off some of the men's pay to supplement his own. Nor can captains provide such kindnesses as wagons for the sick when only in receipt of four shillings. Audley also suggests using only one lieutenant, standard-bearer and sergeant, and removing the vinteners so their wages could be given to a gentleman or worthy soldier of the captain's own band; this would appear as 'dead-pay' later in the century, but was then achieved by cutting the company to 90 men while giving pay for 100. Audley remarks that officers were often chosen by favouritism, not for their military experience.

In 1518 Henry wrote to several captains proposing to appoint some experienced leaders to retain companies ready for action whenever required, paid for by the king, who would decide how many men could be retained. A surviving draft document outlines the details, saying that

ABOVE **The earliest surviving armour of English manufacture is that made around 1515 at the royal workshop at Greenwich for Henry VIII, probably by his Italian or Flemish craftsmen. Decoration was by Paul van Vrelant, the king's harness-gilder. It was used in parades at the 1516 Greenwich tournament and must have been stunning, being entirely engraved, stippled and covered in silver and gold. The horse's bard was probably made in Flanders and was fringed in crimson and gold. Note the size of horse this would have fitted: not a shire but little more than a hunter. (The Board of Trustees of the Armouries, II.5)**

the men would be provided with a coat of Almain armour (imported from Germany, hence the name), a jacket in the green and white royal livery, the king's badge and that of the lord retaining them. They would be mustered once or twice a year but would only receive horses when called, when they would also receive their wages. Statutes against retainers would be enforced if a captain recruited more than required – a safeguard against increasing power. In 1551 the Privy Council nominated a number of captains from their members to make up cavalry contingents from their own retainers, for which the captain received a generous imprest. Some said this was the duke of Northumberland's way of getting extra men to increase his power, but in any case the idea was dropped less than two years later. Nervousness in the Privy Council blocked private suggestions too. In Edward's reign a number of gentlemen, including Sir Thomas Wyatt, came up with the 'King's Militia, or Ordnance of Soldiers', which set out proposals that included avoiding the recruitment into the militia of young fathers or those men worth over 20s per annum, or those unwilling to serve the king. The captain would be chosen annually from a body of likely candidates. However, this proposal fared no better than the rest.

For the 1513 expedition the statute of pay drawn up for Henry VII's proposed invasion of France in 1492 was repeated almost verbatim. Captains were ordered to make sure their men received their wages within six days of the money arriving from the treasurer-at-war. They also had to ensure that the full complement of men agreed with the king were actually present, complete with their colours; prison and forfeiture of goods and chattels awaited those not complying.

In 1539, Sir Richard Morison wrote in the Preface to his translation of *The Strategemes, Sleyghtes, and Policies of Warre* (by Frontinus), one of England's first military books, that the noble captains of England often said they needed no instructions or books to teach them to rough up their enemies.

The commissioners of musters in the shires recruited the militia, which formed the second part of the army. Instructed as to what type of soldier was required and how many, they could endeavour to recruit the desired troop types, resulting in a far more ordered force than did the retained men. Not until the second half of the century would this change be complete, however. When there was not time for issuing commissions the troops were mustered by the sheriffs, who were even more inefficient than the commissioners.

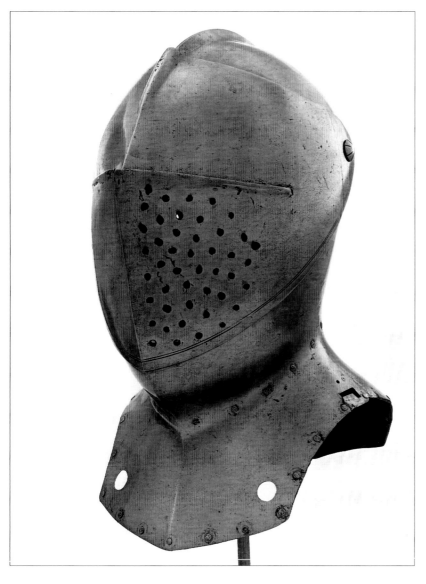

By the 16th century the retinues and militia, though two elements that received pay from their lords or captains respectively, were starting to blend when in battle. Retinues were fragmented as the overall commander saw fit, so that archers were formed together, or billmen or pikemen. It is not known what flag men posted to another area of the army would follow.

Mercenaries were also hired for Continental operations. These were usually Germans ('Almains') and Burgundians. Friction occurred with such men; the Germans in particular seem to have been much less ready to obey orders.

Henry VIII introduced several military reforms, including naval dockyards at Deptford and Woolwich, coastal forts to protect south and east England, an updated armoury in the Tower, an upgraded artillery train and moves to combat a shortage of heavy horses, since only the King's Spears and the nobles were able to serve with armoured mounts, many gentry serving as demi-lances or on foot.

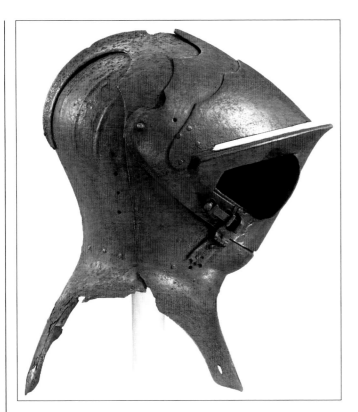

ABOVE **A Flemish or Italian tilting helm of about 1510–20, probably for a form of tournament called Jousts Royal. It was latterly placed in Broadwater Church, Sussex, as part of a memorial probably for Thomas West, Lord La Warre, who died in 1526. (The Board of Trustees of the Armouries, IV.593)**

Edward, Mary and Elizabeth

Commissions to raise troops, held by a chosen person, were also used by Edward VI and Mary, but increasingly rarely by Elizabeth (except in 1586 when six commissioners raised 1,500 volunteers), because of the work of the lord lieutenant (the lieutenant of Henry VIII's time). Elizabeth only issued indentures for a man to lead troops to their port of embarkation. The retinues raised by landowners were no longer used. Regular forces like Edward VI's 'gendarmery' did not reappear. The two royal guards and the militia alone survived.

In 1558 Mary abolished the Statute of Winchester. Now all those with land of £1,000 value or more per year were to keep the following, all of which was to be inventoried and inspected on occasion and none sold:

six horses for demi-lances, three of which should have harness and armour for the rider; ten horses for light horsemen, together with harness and armour for the riders; 40 corselets (infantry cuirasses with full arms, tassets and open helmets); 40 lighter armours for foot ('Almain rivets'), or 40 coats of plates or brigandines; 40 pikes; 30 longbows, each with 24 arrows; 30 light steel caps; 20 bills and halberds; 20 arquebuses; 20 morions.

Those with less income had a suitably reduced burden: men with £5–£10 per year had to provide one coat of plates, one bill or halberd, one bow with arrows and one light helmet.

In 1585 the cost of a horseman was assessed at £25 and the clergy was ordered to raise £25,000 to fund the English force.

The constant need for expeditions gave little pause for any radical alteration in the army structure but, even if it had, the huge costs of maintaining English forces could barely have stood the increased expenditure. There is little evidence that the funds necessary to uphold a standing paid force could easily have been prised out of the populace either, regardless of the release from threats of conscription this would entail. Any nobleman who hinted at private forces, such as Essex, risked accusations of treason. Elizabeth could not, as her father had done, physically take part in military affairs and give opinions based on experience.

Generals, according to Barnaby Rich and Robert Barret, had to be of noble birth in order to command the respect of their men. However, Matthew Sutcliffe pointed out that this could lead to young, inexperienced men being chosen, or worse, those with little military ability. It was a throwback to earlier centuries that the nobility earned its position in society by leading in war; moreover, lingering feudal memories would not

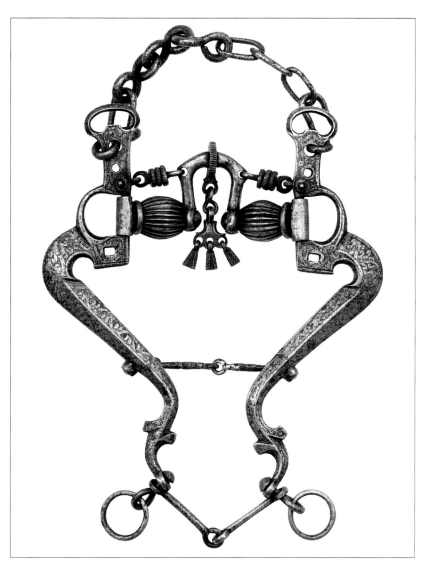

tolerate ordinary men in high rank. This persisted until the end of the 16th century and the Queen, advised by her nobles and with a similar mindset, appointed generals who, on the whole, were not of top quality. Generals also ruled in the Netherlands and as lord deputies in Ireland. Lord Mountjoy was perhaps the most able general of Elizabeth's reign – he proved his skills when sent to deal with Ireland and showed a modern efficient approach rather than the chivalry still practised elsewhere. The earl of Essex sometimes showed great leadership and his courage in battle was not questioned, but he could also make mistakes. He, like the far less able Leicester, was quite willing to put his private affairs first, ending up on the scaffold for treason. The unwillingness of high-ranking nobles to commit themselves to their military tasks was a great drawback. It was sometimes compounded by their being restrained by the orders emanating from the Queen or Privy Council, neither of which was actually in the field.

The high marshal was second-in-command, in charge of justice and camp management. Under him came the provost marshal, either the army officer or the peace officer. A general or lieutenant general of the

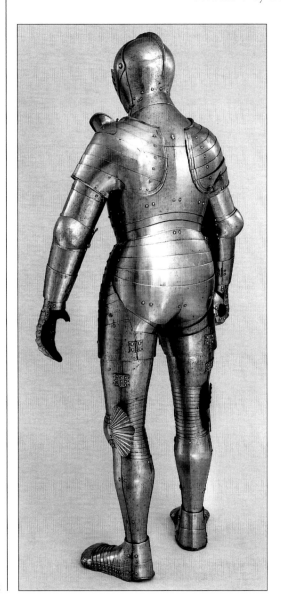

infantry usually took part, and similarly a general of horse, both ranked just below the high marshal. The master of the ordnance was in charge of the stores. He had his own company to guard the guns, which he commanded in action, and controlled ancillary groups such as wheelwrights and pioneers. Below these ranks came numerous lesser officers, such as the forage-master. The sergeant-major (or sergeant-general or sergeant-major-major) was a rank created to connect the general to his captains of companies; to do this the sergeant-major had four corporals of the field, one for each 'battle' (van, main and rear) and one spare.

Finally, after about 1572 (when volunteers went to the Netherlands) and in imitation of Continental armies, English forces adopted the regiment, comprising groups of companies under a colonel. Some, such as Sir John Smythe, a practised soldier, disliked smaller-sized regiments because they needed more officers. However, captains returning from the Low Countries wanted small regiments, and even Continental ones were reducing from 5,000 to 3,000. English regiments reduced from 4,000 to around 1,000-strong, with up to seven companies of about 150–200 men. The sergeant-major-general now contended with colonels ranking far higher than captains. Cavalry companies settled at about 100 men. These paper estimates, however, tended not to be borne out in practice. Captains in the Low Countries dismissed eager men and pocketed their pay. In fact, captains had a reputation for feathering their nests at the expense of army efficiency, a topic that did not go unnoticed by Sir John Smythe. Some unscrupulous captains sent men on hopeless or suicidal missions so they could pocket their pay, or to remove junior officers they detested. Their men had poor uniforms and lost rations so they had to forage for themselves. They sold companies or rented them to their lieutenants. The lieutenant deputised for the captain; the ensign-bearer was of gentle birth and was expected to step in if both captain and lieutenant fell.

The lord lieutenant took over leadership of the militia from the sheriff. There were perhaps between 200,000 and 250,000 men between 16 and 60 years old eligible for the county militia, but only about 20,000 were chosen. Men for special training were now formed into the Trained Bands and where possible exempted from overseas service. This meant that instead of training gentlemen, farmers, yeomen of good stock and labourers, the bands became a hidey-hole for those avoiding foreign service. 'Untrained men' covered conscripts and volunteers. Of the latter, the gentlemen volunteers were a small group (roughly four per company), presumably with an eye to becoming captains. Conscripts, however, included labourers and criminals. Smythe asserted that time wasters made sure they were elsewhere when a levy was made. Sir John

Norreys said such people impaired efficiency. For Ireland the question arose of whether to recruit Irishmen. They received a lower wage, but might often desert, taking equipment, tactical knowledge and sometimes Englishmen with them.

Bow versus bullets

Arguments raged as to whether or not to keep the bow. Sir Roger Williams reckoned that one musketeer was worth three bowmen, while Sir John Smythe was vehemently in favour of the latter. The Privy Council tried in 1569 to make provision for guns but made no headway against popular opinion. Finally in 1595 it took the bold step of ending the use of bows in the armed forces.

TRAINING

From boyhood

By 1500, men of knightly rank did not always wish to fight, and not everyone had come from a background of mounted warriors. There were plenty of other activities, such as running estates, farming, mercantile interests in towns, local government and attending parliament as knights of the shire. Some were naturally attracted to the battlefield, however. Peter Carew, born of a knightly family in 1514, kept playing truant from grammar school, even when his father coupled him to his hound as a lesson. Faring no better at St Paul's school, his father shunted him off as a page to a French friend, but he was so bad that he was made a muleteer until rescued by a relative (a Carew of Haccombe) en route to the siege of Pavia. This relative died on the way, so Peter joined the marquess of Saluzzo, who was killed at the battle of Pavia. Peter then changed sides and was recruited by the Prince of Orange, who was soon also killed. The prince's sister, knowing Peter was homesick, sent him with letters to Henry VIII, who took him into service, impressed by his riding and fluency in French. In 1532 Carew became a gentleman of the Privy Chamber, and was knighted for services at Tre'port in 1544. Three years later he was sheriff of Devonshire and in 1549 perhaps overstepped his duties in putting down the insurrection against the Common Prayer. In 1564–65 he captained a fleet commanded to sweep the western Channel and Irish Sea of pirates. Carew sat on committees concerned with ships, munitions, customs revenues and the defences of the

BELOW **This tonlet armour for foot combats was put together at Greenwich for Henry VIII after the French changed the rules of the tournament planned for the Field of Cloth of Gold. The skirt (tonlet) has leathers riveted on the inner side so that the individual lames can move; the whole can be completely collapsed. It was made partly from existing pieces, the whole then etched en suite. There are signs of haste; for example, the helmet is a great basinet for the tourney that has had a pierced bar welded inside to narrow the vision sights. The gauntlets are associated. (The Board of Trustees of the Armouries, II.7)**

Tower of London. In 1572 he acted as constable of the Tower. He dabbled in architecture and claimed lands in Ireland, and three times served there.

Boys from noble houses might be sent to other households to train as squires, but some men who were knighted for bravery entered the court circle for other reasons and ended up fighting for the king. Sir Humphrey Gilbert (*c.*1537–83) made a telling statement in his outline for an academy in London to teach the sons of nobles and gentlemen: they should study Latin language and literature, philosophy, law, contemporary history, oratory, heraldry and courtliness. The art of war meant learning mathematics, engineering, ballistics and military theory, all equally as useful as skill with lance and sword.

Fewer knights and castles

In Elizabeth's reign the bestowing of knighthoods was deliberately curtailed. Leicester ignored this and made 14 new knights in a single day. Elizabeth then set out that only those with good social standing and finances, or who had proven themselves by some outstanding act of bravery, should warrant being knighted. The Privy Council came to expect all candidates' names to be submitted for approval and by the time of the Queen's death the generals hardly dubbed knights at all any more.

Castles were now becoming redundant, as much from a desire for more comfort as from the effects of gunpowder. However, men still trained in courtyards or else in the grounds of their country house. Teaching a man to wear armour differed little from how it was done in previous centuries. Any man of knightly status could ride but he must

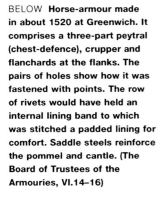

BELOW **Horse-armour made in about 1520 at Greenwich. It comprises a three-part peytral (chest-defence), crupper and flanchards at the flanks. The pairs of holes show how it was fastened with points. The row of rivets would have held an internal lining band to which was stitched a padded lining for comfort. Saddle steels reinforce the pommel and cantle. (The Board of Trustees of the Armouries, VI.14–16)**

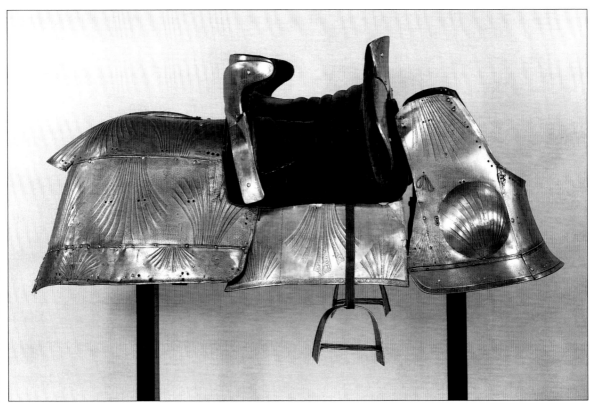

learn to ride a warhorse in armour, and to control it with his legs while using weapons. Charging a dummy called the quintain helped steady the aim and prepare the body for the jarring collision that occurred when a lance struck it. Some quintains may still have consisted of a pivoting arm, one end with a target, the other a sack of sand or a weight that swung round on striking the target to clout anyone not swift enough to avoid it. Running at the ring, a metal ring suspended from a frame, needed a keen eye to pass the lance point through it.

The tournament

Even if many rarely fought in earnest, there was still the tournament in which to impress the sovereign. In London there were lists (arenas for jousting) at Westminster until a fire occurred in 1512, after which all the tournaments in England took place at the Palace of Placentia at Greenwich. A new royal residence at Whitehall in 1533 saw a transfer to this venue and few tournaments were held at Greenwich thereafter. Occasional tournaments were held at Richmond Palace and one at the Tower of London in 1501, whilst a few were held at Hampton Court in Mary's reign; on 29 December 1557 half the contestants were dressed in the Almain (German) fashion and half in Spanish. Other tiltyards elsewhere in the country were occasionally used. Henry VIII was a keen jouster and those who wished to be at the centre of things did well to follow his lead. Queen Elizabeth attended tournaments, notably the Accession Day tilts each November, so those currying favour needed to hone their skills.

The tourney was a group combat, or one between two opponents, each with blunted swords. Foot combat was less hazardous than in earlier centuries since a barrier divided the contestants, so much so that leg-armour was not necessary; blows below the barrier were forbidden. A long spear was used, or sometimes a sword. Jousting was popular but despite special extra tilt pieces, a high barrier to prevent collisions (the tilt), and fluted, hollow lances with blunted points, accidents could still occur. On one occasion Henry VIII forgot to close his helmet and the shower of long wooden splinters that filled his headpiece when his opponent's lance broke on him could have blinded or killed him; luckily (especially for his opponent) he was unhurt and good humoured.

BELOW **The Westminster Tournament Roll was made to commemorate the 1511 tournament held at Westminster. Queen Catherine of Aragon watches with her ladies from a decorated stand as Henry VIII jousts. His trapper bears a heart with the words 'Coeur Loyall' (Loyal Heart) and he is shown breaking his lance against his opponent – although the score cheques show that in reality this did not happen. Others wait their turn, wearing cloth bases over their armour and with frog-mouthed jousting helms stapled to their cuirasses. (The College of Arms)**

Martial skill was just one aspect of the tournament: poetry and allegory flattering the sovereign was all useful material for those in the court. At Sir Henry Lee's entertainment at Woodstock in 1575, Elizabeth saw two mounted knights as she arrived, battling for their ladies' honour in a staged set piece.

APPEARANCE AND DRESS

Armour

Men of rank wore full harness of steel that covered them from top to toe. Initially this might not differ from that worn at the end of the 15th century, a western European style derived from Italian forms with some German influences.

Sabatons (foot armour) sported more rounded toes as they moved towards a broad, bear's paw style. The lower edge of the greave now extended down to cover the back of the heel, usually with a slot up the back to accommodate the spur arm. Instead of straps and buckles the two halves of the greave were now closed by studs springing into holes in the other plate and sometimes further secured by pivot hooks. The lower lame of the poleyn (knee armour) was now cut off straight and grew smaller. The side

wing of the poleyn was at first large with a V-shaped indent, but after the mid-century it grew smaller and by about 1570 had become almost insignificant. From about 1510 the hinged side-plate of the cuisse (thigh armour) was usually changed to an extension of the main plate, but after 1550 grew smaller and then vanished. On the arms, the vambrace (from the wrist to the elbow) was now attached permanently to the pauldron (shoulder armour) or else laced to the arming doublet and the pauldron connected by a strap buckled round the turner of the upper cannon. The large couter on the elbow, which had often been laced to the arming doublet separately, was now attached to the upper and lower cannons by internal leathers and sometimes to the shoulder-defence as well. Until about 1560 some arm-defences had small cup-shaped projections riveted to the upper end of the lower cannon below the couter. Gauntlets, which had commonly been of mitten form, began to be provided with complete fingers after about 1530, and at the same time longer cuffs, more pointed and bell-shaped, came into fashion. The collar had become common by 1520 and might be used to connect the pauldrons by straps.

In the 1540s the waistline of the breastplate began to dip downwards slightly. Twenty years later this had become a point that in the 1570s became the peascod (or 'long-bellied' form) in imitation of fashionable civilian doublets. The following decade saw this style become even more prominent until it nearly reached the crutch. From about 1510 the edges that had previously been turned outwards now turned inwards and were sometimes decorated with roping, though plain angled edges were still seen until about 1570, unlike in the rest of Europe. Frequently recessed borders accompanied these edges. The backplate was often of one piece and flanged at the bottom to take a culet (defence for the rump).

The steel fauld (skirt) of the breast was provided with hanging tassets. At first Gothic-style single-plate tassets remained in use but from 1510 laminated versions, usually rectangular with rounded corners, became increasingly popular, and had replaced the older style by about 1530.

In the last quarter of century the waistcoat cuirass appeared, often with imitation steel buttons. Two halves were hinged to a strip up the back and fastened in front, usually with studs secured by pivot hooks.

Helmets

The sallet and armet helmets of the late 15th century remained in use in some instances for about 20 years. The sallet became more rounded, sometimes with a bellows visor. New forms of armet and other helmet types superseded it. All helmets tended to have a low comb from about 1510 to 1530 (roped for the last ten years); in a few instances the apex was instead drawn up to a quadrangular point that might have an acorn finial. Combs grew larger thereafter but reduced again late in the century. The visor, fitted with a removable pin in each arm, was replaced by an arm pivoted via a screw and internal nut, or sometimes pierced and held by an internal linchpin. A plume holder was now riveted to the base of the skull at the rear, thus replacing the hole in the skull for a crest holder. The plume was sometimes further secured by piercing one or two small holes through the comb to allow binding. The close-helmet developed soon after 1500 from a form of sallet with attached bevor. This was shaped to the head and made in two sections, skull and bevor, the latter pivoting either side of the brow at the same point as the visor that now only covered the opening left by the bevor. When closed the two halves were secured by pivot hooks through pierced staples or sometimes by a sprung stud (attached inside to a strip of springy metal and depressed by another stud on the strip).

Until about 1530 the 'sparrow's beak' visor was popular. Thence the visor became split horizontally into the visor and the upper-bevor (or 'ventail'), into which it fitted. From about 1520 close-helmets were

usually fitted with one or more gorget plates unless they were of the type that rotated on the collar.

The burgonet, an open-faced peaked helmet derived from the sallet, was used by light cavalry and infantry, and was provided in some garnitures for wear as officers. It was also popular for parade armours. After 1510 the burgonet was often accompanied by a buffe, a kind of bevor fitted with gorget plates. Occasionally a morion was worn by infantry officers, with tall skull and pointed brim.

The arming doublet was only lightly quilted, and throughout the century come references to arming bolsters, padded rolls worn round the hips to support the cuirass, and to quilted collars called arming partlets. Pieces of armour might be lined or padded, and from mid-century might be decorated by leather or fabric tabs known as pickadils. Over the armour fabric bases were sometimes worn or, during tournaments or parades, civilian robes.

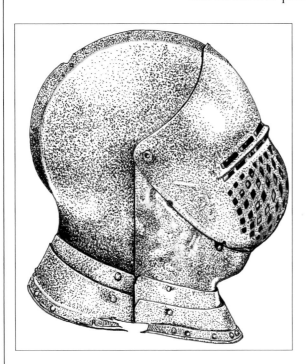

ABOVE **A Greenwich helmet from Southacre Church, Norfolk, with a rounded visor seen from about 1530 to 1540. (Author's illustration)**

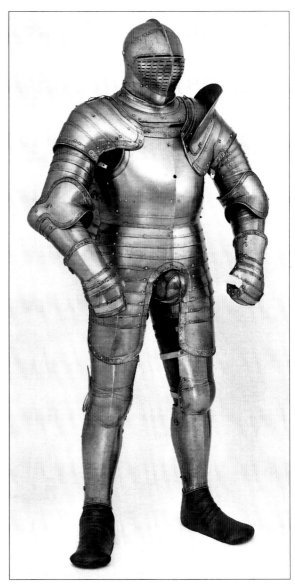

RIGHT **Greenwich armour of Henry VIII, dated 1540, a garniture probably made for the Westminster tournament that year. It has etched and gilt decoration after the school of Holbein. Basically a heavy field armour, extra pieces enabled it to be made up as for tilt, tourney or foot combat. Here it is made for the latter, though it probably had a matching right pauldron without the cutaway for the lance-rest, which was not needed. It has also lost its sabatons and right haute-piece. It may also have been designed to be made up for medium and light field use, but in the absence of all the pieces this is speculative. (The Board of Trustees of the Armouries, II.8)**

The brigandine lined with small tinned plates continued to be quite popular until the second half of the century. The inventory of Edmund Dudley in 1509 shows two rich examples for himself plus 30 fustian-covered examples for his men. Mail coats, consisting of thousands of interlinked riveted rings, might be worn under civilian clothing, either for duelling or as protection against assassination. Mail parts were also worn late in the century by officers as captains of light horse or infantry.

The Greenwich workshop and style

In 1511 Henry VIII set up a small workshop at Greenwich near the royal palace, staffed by a group of Italian craftsmen from Milan, followed by a group of Flemish craftsmen. In 1514 Henry was sent a present by Emperor Maximilian I of a magnificent tonlet armour made by the Innsbruck master armourer, Conrad Seusenhofer. Presenting gifts was a recognised social function for heads of state, but Henry was apparently still unable to reply in kind from English workshops. The following year he brought in the most important group of men, armourers from

LEFT **A crinet or neck-defence for a horse. Made for Henry VIII by his Greenwich workshop in 1544, each lame moves on internal leathers. It is decorated with etched and gilt designs. Below is a matching mitten gauntlet, both pieces from a lost armour. (The Board of Trustees of the Armouries, VI.69)**

ABOVE **A tilting lance traditionally associated with Henry VIII. It is designed to shatter on impact, and to that end is partially hollow inside and fluted on the outside. The leather strip nailed round the butt behind the waisted grip was designed to ram against the lance-rest to prevent the weapon sliding through the armpit. (The Board of Trustees of the Armouries, VII.551)**

Germany itself, the 'Almains'. In 1516 the royal workshop moved to Southwark, but between 1521 and 1525 it was back at Greenwich, where it remained until about 1637. As a royal workshop Greenwich was technically there to provide armours for the king, and the workmanship of the craftsmen would rival the top centres in Europe. Henry had several other armours made, some now surviving only from a few pieces. Under Mary and Elizabeth it would be courtiers who would purchase armours from the royal workshop.

By the second half of the century the Greenwich style had developed. A form of armet that had first appeared in Germany was developed after about 1525, whereby the tail became wider and the cheek-pieces hinged to it at their rear edges, a style seen until about 1615, despite the close-helmet's increasing popularity elsewhere. Greenwich visors had a gracefully curved prow like that of a ship, and for ventilation there were usually vertical slits each pierced by a hole. Other features are discussed in the Plates section.

The garniture

When men of rank wanted to take part in tournaments, they might require armours for several types of contest: the tourney, jousts and foot combats, not to mention harness designed for use in battle either mounted or on foot. All this could be extremely expensive, and around 1500 a new solution was beginning to appear: the garniture. This was in effect a set of interchangeable parts that allowed armours to be made up for a variety of uses. The individual pieces of the garniture were often decorated en suite.

Decoration

Varying degrees of decoration frequently enriched armour worn by men of rank. In the early 16th century this was sometimes done by engraving with a sharp burin (a metal cutting tool with a sharp bevelled point). However, etching was already being used to decorate metal with less effort and would become the main technique, though in the last quarter some armours might be decorated by designs on shaped punches. In etching a mild acid such as vinegar ate away part of the surface to produce the required decoration, after coating the surface to be decorated with a protective 'resist' (wax or paint) and cutting the design through the resist with a needle to expose the metal. The second method, used from about 1510 in Germany and a decade later in Italy, involved coating areas to be left untouched with a resist applied by brush, and only using a needle for fine detail. A granular effect could be obtained by liberally covering a surface with small dots of wax, a typically Germanic style as opposed to the plain ground initially used by the Italians. Thus larger etched areas were more easily achieved, and this became the main way to etch armour. Greenwich armours were at first etched in Italian style but after 1570 in German style, with native English designs.

Etched decoration was frequently enhanced by mercury gilding, an amalgam of gold and mercury being painted on to the desired area and the mercury heated to chase it off, leaving the gold fused to the surface. More rarely gold might be applied as gold leaf, whereby the surface was hatched to make the leaf stick when it was laid on and burnished. Silver foil was also sometimes added this way, the most famous example being

Henry VIII's armour for man and horse of about 1515. Gilding was usually applied to borders or as decorative bands. Sometimes the gilding was only applied to the ground, leaving the raised design in steel, or the ground and the design lines were blackened (more a German feature). The surface might be further enhanced by controlled heating of the steel to produce a beautiful deep blue or russet red. An easier method of colouring was to paint the surface, commonly in black, leaving areas of natural steel to produce what is called 'black-and-white' armour. This was especially popular in Germany but uncommon amongst men of rank in England.

Another uncommon form of decoration was embossing: raising a design by hammering from the underside of the metal. This obviously dispensed with the smooth surface necessary to make weapon points glance off, and was used rather for parade items. One of the best survivals is the so-called Burgundian Bard, a horse-armour gifted to Henry VIII by the Emperor Maximilian. Embossing was also employed to produce the grotesque masks used on some tourney helmet visors, though this was much more popular in Germany. Damascening entailed cutting channels along the design lines and filling these with gold or silver strips hammered into place. Damascening was often used in conjunction with embossing, but the process was rare in England. The practice of applying precious jewels, enamels, or gold or silver plates to helmets was still very occasionally seen in the early 16th century.

Arms

The sword

The sword remained the favoured arm of the gentleman. Military weapons at the beginning of the 16th century still had long thrusting

BELOW **St Mawes Castle in Cornwall, built 1540–43. For defence of the realm, Henry constructed a series of forts such as this one, basically gun platforms with low circular towers and rounded battlements to present a small, deflective target to cannonballs. Unlike a true castle, nobody used it as a home; it simply housed a garrison and commander. (Author's collection)**

blades, but were wide enough to deliver a lethal cut from the sharpened edges. The hilt was still essentially a simple cross, the wooden grip bound in cloth or leather and often overlaid by cords or wire either twined round or in a lattice, to help prevent the weapon slipping in the hand. A pommel at the end helped prevent the hand sliding off but more importantly provided a counterbalance to the blade, so that the point of balance was as near to the hand as possible; this made the sword less point-heavy and less tiring to use. Several styles of pommel had been developed, from a simple disc or flanged wheel to a scent-bottle style. This type of cross-hilt continued to be worn with armour by a few enthusiasts until after the third quarter of the 16th century. However, by the beginning of the century some infantry swords had already developed a half loop or a ring to guard the finger hooked over the blunted first section of blade to assist a swing. This form was then seen on the swords of gentlemen. By mid-century swords usually had finger-rings and side-rings, but frequently lacked the knuckle-guards and displayed none of the diagonal guards popular in Continental Europe. The estoc was also known in England as the tuck. The blade sometimes had three or even four unsharpened sides to produce a very stiff weapon for maximum thrust. Ordinary followers might simply have sword and buckler.

Blades usually came in from Toledo in Spain, northern Italy, or Passau or Solingen in Germany. Smiths put their name or mark on the blade but some added the name of a famous smith or centre of manufacture to fool the unwary. A sword knot of cord or ribbon, forming a loop ending in a tassel, was occasionally added; it could slip

BELOW **An army in battle-order in the time of Henry VIII. Cavalry screen the main bodies. (Permission British Library)**

over the hand to prevent loss. It was sometimes added either through a hole in the pommel or more commonly round the grip.

Wearing the sword

The scabbard was made from two strips of wood covered in leather, cloth or velvet. The covering may sometimes have been made to match a man's clothing, for several are recorded for one sword. A metal chape reinforced the scabbard tip but a locket guarding the mouth was rare. On many scabbards the sides of the mouth were cut away, leaving a piece of the wood at front and back to slip up between the guards and over the ricasso (the dull part of the blade right above the hilt). Elaborate belts were developed to sling the sword from a convenient angle and to prevent the wearer from tripping over it. Early belts followed medieval practice, with three straps or slings to the waist belt, the two rearmost joining the waist belt to the rear; sometimes a single strap here bifurcated to form two connecting points to the scabbard. The front strap usually had an adjusting buckle, and a small hook connecting the strap to a ring on the waist belt became common. However, largely after 1550 the front sling (called a 'side-piece') now crossed the stomach to join the waist belt on the right. The central waist-buckle began to move round to the right hip, and a ring attached to the lower part of a slide replaced the ring on the waist belt. However, some never changed from the left-of-centre attachment. At about the same time the rear scabbard slings were given ring attachments to the waist belt; often now these slings joined at the top and used a single hook. Increasingly, each sling was fitted with a slide and the lower end of the sling, having wrapped round the scabbard, was stitched to the central bar of the slide; the scabbard's weight ensured the loop was pulled tight. In the second half of the century the rear slings became joined into a single broad sling of leather or stuff – the hanger – its lower edge divided into as many as 12 straps with slides, wrapped round the scabbard. The side-piece was permanently attached to a leading corner. Hangers were often embroidered to match costume or sword hilt. At first heater-shaped, at the end of the century round-topped versions appeared. At the turn of the 17th century a few swords were worn with knuckle-guard upwards.

Two cuts in the covering below the mouth allowed smaller scabbards to be inserted that held one or more by-knives and a bodkin. These seem to have sometimes been worn on the inner side or could instead be set in the dagger sheath. The bodkin may have been used to pierce eyelet holes for points. Perhaps in the second quarter of the 16th century a transverse rib developed below the knives, to stop the scabbard sliding through the hanger.

THE ENCAMPMENT OF KING HENRY VIII. AT MARQUISON, JULY MDXLIV.

ENGRAVED FROM A COEVAL PAINTING AT COWDRAY IN SUSSEX, THE SEAT OF LORD VISCOUNT MONTAGUE.

ABOVE **The English camp at Marquison after the storm during the night of 25 July 1544, an engraving from lost murals at Cowdray House, Sussex. The wheeled triangular-covered objects are small artillery pieces called 'shrimps'. (Courtesy of the Director, National Army Museum, London)**

From 1575 the baldric became an alternative way to carry the sword when worn with armour, but it was advisable to wear a waist sash to stop the sword swinging about. In the 1550s and 1560s it was fashionable to wear a matching cloth pouch on the right side, with a metal mount at the mouth, to which was attached the suspension loop. If worn with armour a flap was buttoned over the mouth and the mount discarded.

By the end of the 15th century a sword was increasingly worn with civilian costume and was common after 1530. It now became popular for duelling. The latter had been a way of settling disputes for centuries, but for men of rank it had usually been done in full armour in the lists. Now duels on foot between men in civilian dress became more popular: a way to settle disputes without resorting to expensive equipment. The duelling sword did not need to be as sturdy as a military weapon, since it would be used against an un-armoured opponent; therefore the blade was lighter and grips developed to guard the unprotected hand. The early rapier was simply a long civilian sword whose edged blade might be wider than that of a tuck. It was not until mid-century that the word came to refer to a purely thrusting sword. This move, as opposed to the cut, was now favoured and promoted by Italian fencing masters, where the science of duelling had developed. Those wishing to learn might also consult the manuals such masters produced, and the skill was later also taken up by Spanish masters.

Unlike the military sword, civilian weapons did follow European fashion in developing a more complicated hilt, partly because duellists were un-armoured. Hilts were sometimes simply bright steel, or could be blued by heat treatment or fire-gilt. They might be inlaid with silver plates decorated in relief or with strips along the guards, chiselled or pierced. Engraved silver plates might also be riveted on. The steel could be decorated by chiselling; in the first part of the century a roped design and animal heads were the usual styles. Damascening was sometimes used but counterfeit damascening (inlaying the wire into hatching) was far more common. Encrusting (like damascening but with the precious metal left proud and then engraved or chiselled) first appeared on chiselled hilts mid-century and was the commonest decoration by 1600. Occasionally enamel was employed.

Perhaps the most famous fencing master in England in the later 16th century was the London master, George Silver, who published a treatise entitled *Paradoxes of Defence* in 1599. Silver notes that Italian teachers maintained the English would not hook their forefinger over the cross nor lay the thumb on the blade or the hand on the pommel, because the English hilts lacked protective finger rings; therefore they could not thrust straight. They probably did hook the finger if using an Italian style of hilt.

The opponent's blade might be warded by the left hand or with the cloak wrapped round the arm, which could also be used to envelope the blade. By mid-century, however, a dagger was often carried in the left hand specifically to engage an opponent's sword. The dagger was fitted with a simple cross-guard and a shell-guard or ring-guard for the first finger. A weapon popular during the reign of Henry VIII was the Holbein dagger in fashionable Swiss style. This had a hilt that was shaped like an 'I' made from cast metal and decorated with strapwork and faces. The sheath was of ornamented metal, sometimes of intricate pierced design. By about 1550 a Scottish style of dagger was reportedly popular. A matching sword and dagger might be ordered by wealthier men, the dagger with simple cross-guard and a ring-guard – or, in the second half of the century, a shell – on the outside.

The rapier

When in civilian dress, knights now sometimes wore a rapier. Much ink was spilt at the time in assessing whether the traditional sword or the English tuck was better than these weapons. Sir John Smythe wrote *Instructions, Observations and Orders Mylitarie* in 1591, published four years later. In it he points out that the rapier is too long for a foot soldier to

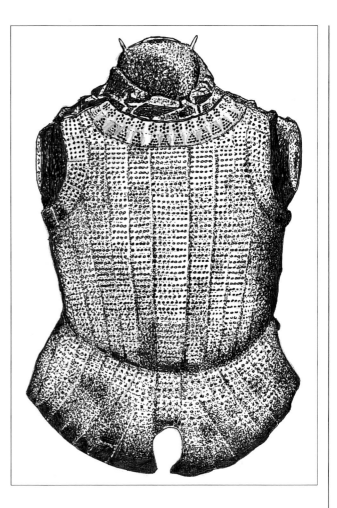

ABOVE **Brigandine of c.1540, probably Italian, in the Metropolitan Museum of Art, New York. Lined with small overlapping plates, men of rank covered the front with rich material such as silk or satin, whilst the rivet heads were of tinned iron or gilt latten. At first it was fastened down the front (or one or both sides) and over the shoulders, by straps and buckles or lacing; some were laced down the front and sides. By the second quarter of the century side and shoulder fastenings were usual. (Author's collection)**

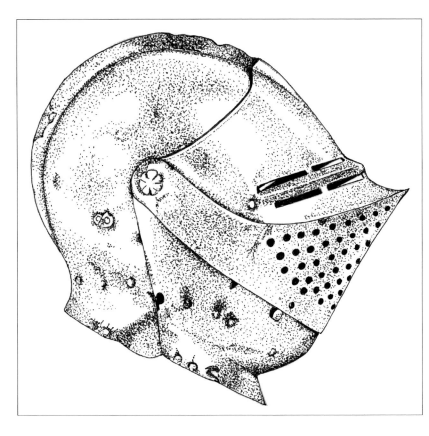

draw in the press of battle or a horseman to draw unless he lets his rein fall, and is not therefore a military weapon. Moreover, the blade was so hard and narrow that it broke when it struck armour. Tucks, however, with their foursquare thrusting blades, he notes as sometimes worn on horseback by men-at-arms and demi-lances, under their thighs in the Hungarian or Turkish manner.

George Silver disliked rapiers, referring to them as 'bird-spits' and, echoing Smythe, he lists all the things they cannot do in battle: pierce a corselet with the point, unlace a helmet, unbuckle armour or cut through pikes. He considers them unsuitable for cutting, excessively long and with inadequate guards. He says that many skilled men using them are wounded because they cannot uncross the weapon without stepping back. Nevertheless, rapiers were becoming popular for wear with civilian dress and their owners had to be trained in their use. For this they went to the foreign fencing masters who were setting up schools in London and who may have provided a further reason for Silver's hostility to the new weapon.

The *Articles for the due execution of the Statutes of Apparell,* of 6 May 1562, was based on a proclamation of 1557. Nobody under the rank of knight was to wear gilt spurs or damascened or gilt sword, rapier or dagger, upon pain of forfeiture and imprisonment and fine. It also stated that no man was to wear a sword, rapier or other weapon over 'one yard and halfe a quarter of blade, at the vttermost: neither any Dagger aboue the length of xii inches in blade: neither any Buckler, with a sharpe point, or with any point aboue two ynches of length'. Forfeiture, imprisonment and fine were the penalty. Officers were empowered to cut down blades exceeding permitted lengths and might be stationed at town gates; in 1580 they nearly caused a diplomatic incident when they stopped the French ambassador at the bars at Smithfield, to the fury of the Queen.

Daggers and other weapons

Daggers were carried in a sheath on the right side, two staples on the locket attaching to the waist belt. After about 1560 the dagger was usually worn well back. In some cases the locket had a ring either side for two cords with a tassel, 'a venecian tassel of sylke' as Thomas Becon calls it mid-century. Robert, Earl of Leicester, had cords of silver and gold, blue and gold, black and gold, and crimson silk and gold with matching tassels. Chains, ribbons or a large bow were also seen. Some lockets were also made to take by-knives and a bodkin.

False scabbards were common, being leather cases made to cover a sword or rapier scabbard tightly but did not enclose the hilt itself.

The hand-and-a-half-sword, or bastard sword, continued in use but now even longer weapons were becoming more common. The fearsome-looking two-hand sword was largely designed for infantry use in cutting through ranks of pike shafts to allow those following to break into the enemy formation. The base of the blade might be furnished with two lugs to stop an enemy weapon sliding down, this portion often covered in leather to provide a grip.

The horseman's hammer now often had a steel shaft to prevent cutting, fitted with a hammer-head backed by a diamond-sectioned spike. Maces were more rare, fitted with triangular or curved tubular flanges. Richer examples might be decorated, for example with silver or gold damascening on a blued or russeted ground.

The two royal bodyguards, the Gentlemen-at-Arms and the Yeomen of the Guard, carried pollaxes and partisans respectively on State occasions.

Firearms

The principal gun used by the gentry was the wheellock, which used the spinning action of an abrasive wheel against a piece of iron pyrites to create sparks. The great advantage of the wheellock was that it could be wound up ready for action so that the pistol could be discharged swiftly. For military use a pair of pistols was carried in leather holsters at the saddle bow, but a man of rank would only use these when serving as a captain of cavalry. The other form of lock was the snaphance, in which a flint struck the face of a steel mounted on a pivoted arm. This form of ignition would eventually be modified by amalgamating the

pan cover with the steel, to form the flintlock. The snaphance was cheaper than the wheellock, which also had the disadvantage of having the main moving parts inside the breech, making servicing difficult in the field, especially as the parts could break if roughly handled. The English did not at first take up the idea of the cartridge, whereby the powder and ball were tied in a paper cartridge, though from mid-century it began to appear in mainland Europe.

Novelty combination weapons were very occasionally carried, such as swords fitted with a small pistol in the hilt, or horseman's hammers combined with a wheellock pistol similarly firing through the end of the grip.

Sumptuary laws of Henry VIII

Sumptuary laws were designed to ensure that men's position in society was reflected in their dress and appearance. Henry VIII produced the following version of the laws:

> None shall wear ... cloth of gold or silver, or silk of purple colour ... except ... Earls, all above that rank, and Knights of the King

RIGHT **A Greenwich garniture for Henry Herbert, Earl of Pembroke, made 1550–57. The cuirass has an anime breastplate and he wears a close helmet of burgonet form. This is the most complete Greenwich garniture to survive. Originally the steel was bright, being decorated with etching and gilding. (Glasgow City Council [Museums])**

(and then only in their mantles). None shall wear … cloth of gold or silver, tinselled satin, silk, cloth mixed or embroidered with gold or silver, or foreign woollen cloth … except … Barons, all above that rank, Knights of the Garter, and Privy Councillors. None shall wear … any lace of gold or silver, lace mixed with gold or silver, silk, spurs, swords, rapiers, daggers, buckles, or studs with gold, silver or gilt … except … Baron's Sons, all above that rank, Gentlemen attending the Queen, Knights and Captains. None shall wear … velvet in gowns, cloaks, coats, or upper garments, or embroidery with silk, or hose of silk … except … Knights, all above that rank, and their heirs apparent. None shall wear … velvet, satin, damask, taffeta, or grosgrain in gowns, cloaks, coats, or upper garments, or velvet in their jerkins, hose or doublets … except … Knight's Eldest Sons and all above that rank.

Horses

Henry VII had banned the sale of good stock abroad in 1495, blaming the Yorkists for this and so causing a shortage of good mounts. At the beginning of the 16th century horses bred for war were similar to those of the previous century, stallions that were deep-chested for good windage, with solid quarters and a thick neck yet still reasonably nimble. They were not especially large by today's standards: one look at the armour made in about 1515 for a horse of Henry VIII confirms that in height it was no more than a hunter. In order to highlight his importance in foreign eyes especially, Henry VIII sent men to find horses in Italy. For the Field of Cloth of Gold in 1520 Henry chose a Neapolitan, but his stables also contained a Frieslander bay from the duke of Mantua, a horse of the breed of Isabella, Duchess of Milan, from the duke of Ferrara and 25 Spanish mounts from Emperor Charles V.

Acts were passed to force every owner of an enclosed park to keep two mares in it, each at least of 13 hands (1535), to forbid any stallion less than 15 hands and over the age of two from being placed in areas where mares and fillies were kept (1540) and to force the nobility to keep specific quotas of horses (1541–42). These latter acts included archbishops and dukes (seven trotting horses for the saddle, each at least three years old and 14 hands high); marquesses, earls and bishops with an income of £1,000 or more (five of these trotting horses);

BELOW **Armour of a demi-lance, a three-quarter harness made for the earl of Pembroke, at Greenwich in about 1555. (The Board of Trustees of the Armouries, II.137)**

viscounts and barons with an income of £1,000 (three trotting horses); and those with incomes of 500 marks (two trotting horses). Anyone with an income of £100 per year, whose wife wore a silk gown or any French hood or bonnet of velvet, 'with any habiliment, paste, or egg of gold, pearl or stone, or any chain of gold about their neck or in their partlets, or in any apparel of their body' also had to maintain such a trotting horse. The Gentlemen Pensioners created by Henry also had to keep studs, and many received parks taken from dissolved monasteries. Sir Nicholas Arnold received such a park at Highnam, seized from Gloucester, where he maintained Neapolitan warhorses and animals from Flanders. Maintaining a stud was not cheap, not least because fencing, gates and walls had to be maintained to ensure that only desired stallions covered the mares. Several of the Pensioners wrote treatises on horse breeding and management that reveal Italian ways of thinking that were themselves based on Xenophon's *Hippike*. Other men of position also favoured Italian methods to manage their horses – Robert Dudley, Earl of Leicester, imported a Pavian riding-master, Claudio Corte, during his time as Master of Horse (1558–81) and one Pensioner, Sir Thomas Bedingfield, translated Corte's work. Federigo Grisone published his *Rules of Horsemanship* in Naples (1550); this was translated in England and presented to Dudley. However, Elizabeth railed against poor horse breeding and issued several proclamations.

The new ideas of less powerful but more agile horses for war were gaining ground but never in the 16th century ousted the traditional warhorse that carried fully armoured men, especially in the tilt. More emphasis was now placed on teaching movements such as the *croupade* where the back kick is performed when the animal has jumped into the air. This new 'management' was increasingly popular; Corte advocated the use of rings to train and exercise horses: 'for skirmish, for battell, and for combate, either offending or defending. It is also a comelie sight in the rider, and standeth him in steed for the exercise of the turneie, and all other feates of armes.' Veterinary medicine was now making progress in England, largely thanks to the enquiring mind of an illiterate groom in the service of gentlemen, Christopher Clifford, who wrote (one assumes with help) *The Schoole of Horsemanship*, published in 1585. By the end of the century Arabs, Barbs or Spanish Jennets were increasingly used in European studs to produce elegant yet swift, strong mounts.

LIFE ON CAMPAIGN

Abroad

Knights and lords could find themselves campaigning in several theatres: in 1511 Thomas, Lord Darcy, was sent with about 1,500 archers to assist Ferdinand against the Moors of Barbary (a waste of time). The experienced Sir Edward Poynings, Warden of the Cinque Ports and former Lord Deputy of Ireland, did well when ordered to assist Margaret of Savoy (Maximilian's daughter) against the duke of Guelders. Men of rank might also be contracted for special duties: Willoughby in 1512 was primarily nominated to be master of the ordnance and artillery. Knights also led scouting parties of cavalry, as in 1513 when Sir John Neville espied the French gathering to launch a relief attempt during the siege

of Thérouanne, their company being blundered into by the earl of
Essex and Sir John Peachy while Neville was reporting his findings. In
Mary's reign a force under William Herbert, first Earl of Pembroke, was
sent to aid the Spanish against a French army. The force included such
men as Lord Bray, Ambrose and Robert Dudley, Sir Nicholas
Throckmorton, the second earl of Bedford and Sir Peter Carew, but was
too late for the battle of St Quentin on 10 August, when the French were
defeated. However, this force played a significant role in the siege of the
city that followed. In 1586 Sir Philip Sidney, appointed by Elizabeth to
be governor of Flushing in the Netherlands, died of a musket wound in
the thigh received at a skirmish against the Spanish at Zutphen.

On the march

Roger Williams in his *Briefe Discourse* says that few captains would force
men to march over 15 miles without a break. Troops marched in various
formations but it is difficult to know if the flank guards marched in line
abreast or in column. Certainly the three wards, van, middle and rear,
were used even when transporting the army across the Channel. It made
it easier to unload large numbers of men from one ward and have them
move off before the next batch of ships arrived. In open country three
regiments followed one another, preceded by shot, flanked by archers
and columns of artillery, while cavalry screened the army. If a retreat was
necessary, Audley's advice was to face the enemy. Turning and running
was asking to be cut up without being able to defend oneself.

Experiences in the field depended on forward planning and the
stamp of the leaders. Thomas Grey, Marquess of Dorset, sent by Henry to
join Ferdinand's troops in the invasion of Guienne (1511), was
incompetent: food and pay were lacking and there was near mutiny (also

because Ferdinand changed his mind). At the inquest the leaders were kept on their knees until they begged to stand, and were proved guilty.

Rations and supply

The army's rations highlighted differences in rank. The ordinary soldiers ate the hardest bread, multi-coloured butter and flyblown meat. The knights and lords ate the finer white bread and fresher butter and meat. While they might drink fine wines, the rank and file were sustained on daily rations of beer and ale, safer to drink than water. However, over-imbibing in Spain led to a revolt by men under Dorset while on an expedition in 1512. The armies that invaded the Continent were too large to live off the land alone and thus supply trains were a necessity. Men of rank found themselves in charge of escorting these vital parts of Henry's military machine, and not without incident, for the French chose to target them instead of risking pitched battle. In 1513 daily convoys from Calais supplied the English van and rear camped near Thérouanne, as they waited for the arrival of the middle ward, one of which convoys was seized.

RIGHT **A close-burgonet made at Greenwich _c_.1555. This is a hybrid form with elements of both close-helmet and burgonet helmet styles. (The Board of Trustees of the Armouries, IV.604)**

Knight, *c.*1525

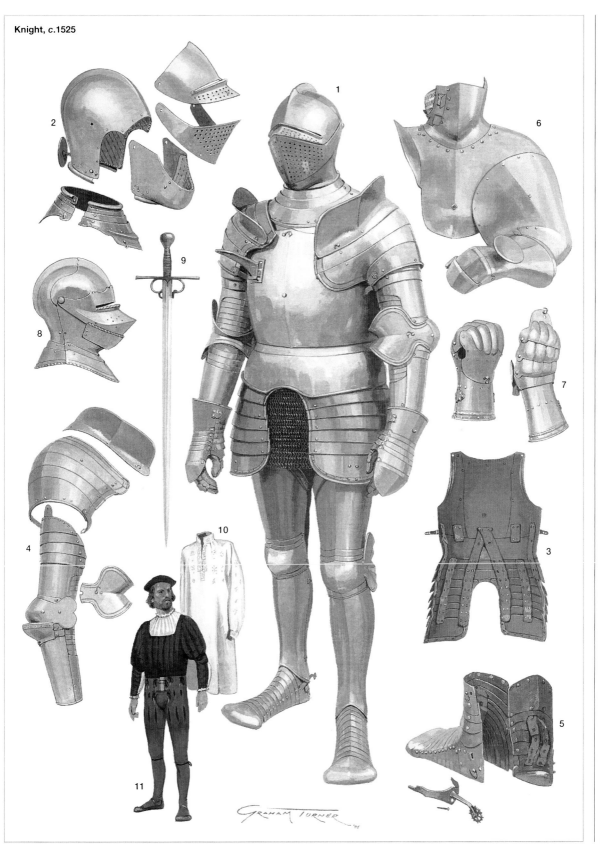

A

The battle of the Spurs, 16 August 1513

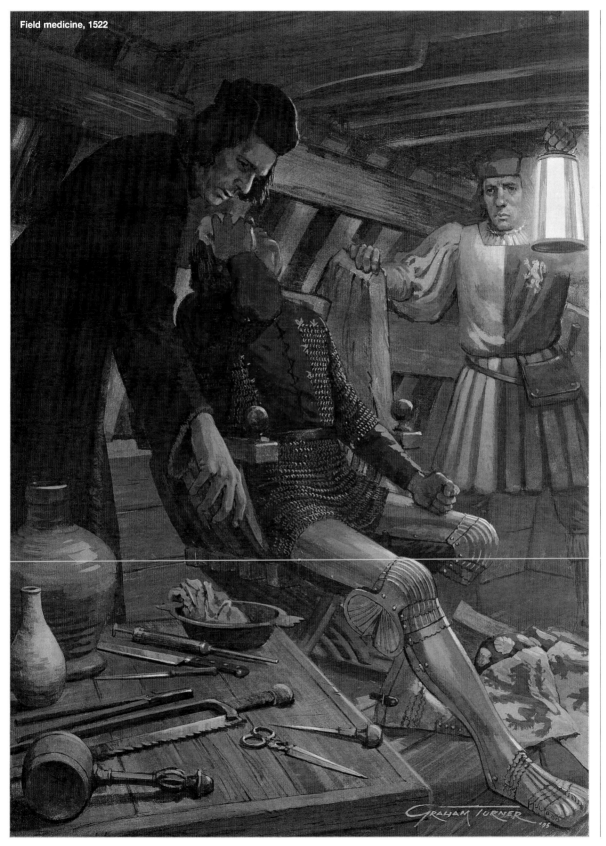

Field medicine, 1522

C

Knight, *c.*1550

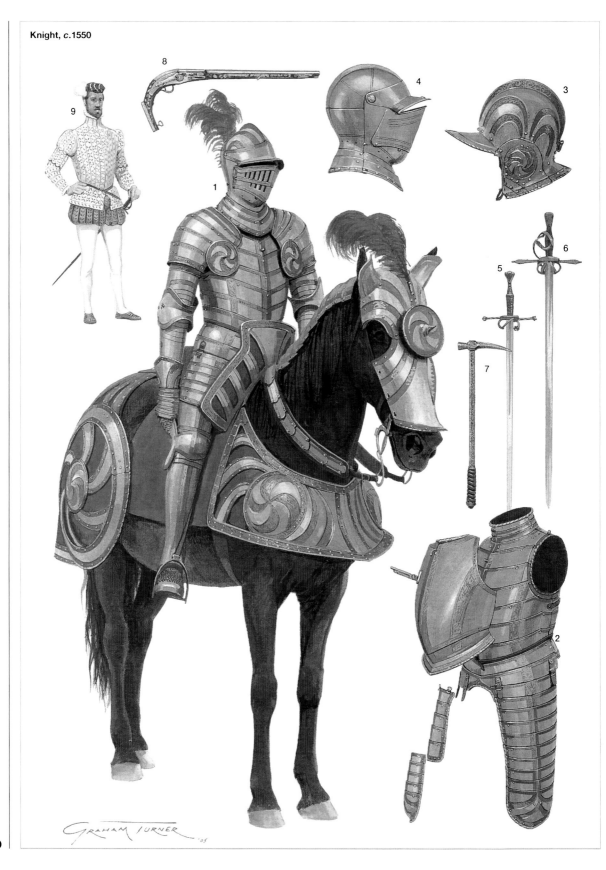

Elizabethan hunting scene

E

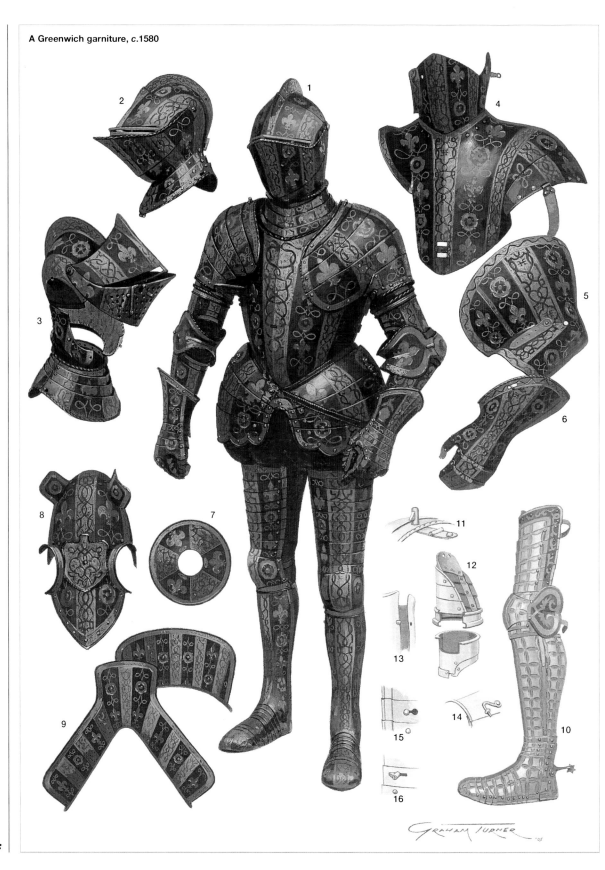

A Greenwich garniture, c.1580

F

The Accession Day tilts, c.1586

G

Knight, c.1590

1

2

3

4

5

6

7

8

9

10

GRAHAM TURNER
'05

H

In Elizabeth's reign food supply remained a problem. Keeping garrisons fed in Ireland or the Netherlands was difficult. As soon as Leicester arrived in the Low Countries he sent to England for rations so that food was available in case there were weather problems later with short notice requests.

Replacing deserters, or sick or deceased soldiers, was a headache for captains. Short campaigns were less of a problem than areas in permanent occupation, such as Ireland or the Netherlands, where levies had to be sent from England. Walsingham reckoned that about 1,000 men could be found by recruiting English volunteers from Dutch regiments. In 1594 the Privy Council ruled that the captain should be responsible for immediate replacement of anyone leaving the company. Funding for a new man was provided as a man's pay for a month and came from fines taken for deficiencies of equipment. However, this replacement had to take place within two months and the recruit be notified to the muster master. The uniform allowance for the lost soldier was also provided (gauged at the beginning of the season to his departure date) to pay for equipment and arms. Wherever possible this money was only paid out once the new man was with the company. In Ireland civilians were offered enrolment so numbers were not a problem, except that the companies lacked English soldiers.

Clothing of levies depended partly on the lord lieutenant. The white coats of Henry VIII's time gave way to uniforms of many hues; costs and provision of coats was down to the county. In the Netherlands officers had a doublet of Milan fustian faced with taffeta, a pair of broadcloth Venetians trimmed with silk and lined with cotton and linen, and worsted stockings. For winter wear there was a broadcloth cassock lined with baize and faced with taffeta. Buckhurst thought that only colonels and above should be allowed silk and lace; captains should make do with fustian, cloth and canvas and spend on arms rather than clothing. Digges and Cecil commented adversely on the captains' love of silks and jewels. Early in Elizabeth's reign 'coat money' was paid for uniform and 'conduct money' for expenses from point of assembly to point of embarkation. Corruption was noted in many places – some captains purloined clothing allowances. Eventually they were stopped from being involved in uniform distribution.

Corruption in the army

Corruption was the biggest drawback to making Elizabeth's army noteworthy; it was found from the highest to the lowest levels, but was endemic amongst the officers, including men of rank. The Council did increasingly monitor local authorities, particularly after 1585 and Elizabeth's entry

into the war in Europe. Tougher demands were balanced by more concern for ordinary soldiers. Musters gave captains opportunities for selling releases. Lords lieutenant organised musters but where there were none commissioners were deferred to, selected from justices of the peace and other prominent gentlemen and commissioned by the Queen with a detailed set of instructions. Unfortunately captains used their time to enrich themselves and made it hard for any honest muster-master. It was for service in Ireland that deception was greatest. After levying in Chester and once clear of the area, a captain exacted payments from the new recruits and left them with their equipment (also probably paid for); he now had their conduct money as well. He then briefly hired the correct number of 'soldiers' from local civilians in order to pass muster; the equipment was returned to await the next muster. The captain then went to Ireland and could try for passage money as well; shortfalls – every place in a company in some cases – were covered up for musters by drawing on other companies or engaging native Irishmen. Pay, known as imprests, was also in the captain's hands, given weekly as a proportion that was made up every six months. The trouble was that the old feudal idea of men in control of their contingents had not been shaken off, despite re-organisation in the army where the state was in charge of recruitment and wages. Corruption went to high levels: Sir George

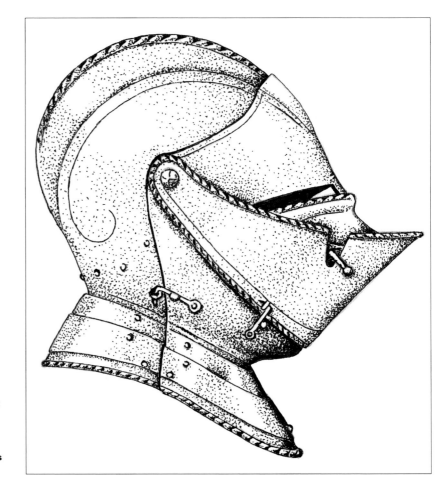

RIGHT **A close-helmet of c.1570 probably evolving from a 'sparrow's-beak' form (see Plate A). Both were to be found in English churches and suggest English work under Italian influence. Staples and sneck hooks are generally used to secure movable pieces. (Author's collection)**

Carey was dabbling in fraud in Ireland, while Sir Henry Sidney was arranging for a number of new servants to be paid out of the concordatum fund that was designed for unexpected payments but not of the type Sir Henry had in mind.

The corruptions of captains and others were on the agenda in the 1589 Normandy campaign, with strict penalties for those caught. However, the brisk muster by Lord Buckhurst came to nought when the troops found themselves stuck in camp because the embarkation was postponed. Then there was the farcical argument by Captain Cosbie that the men should all look similarly smart with new Spanish morions instead of the Italian form with high crest while – even more shocking – some were black while others were not. The pikemen, moreover, had not been supplied with peascod breastplates. So indignant was he that he had the troops throw away their arm defences and only carry helmet and cuirass. Cosbie even moaned about the lack of stockings in Sussex.

Discipline in Tudor armies

Discipline was quite high in the Tudor army of 1513. The penalties for misdemeanours such as falling asleep on duty were usually simple fines, however, and nothing like the torture and execution that appears in Elizabeth's reign. Much of the trouble seemed to stem from the German troops under Henry's command. On 15 August there was a riot in the camp near Aire-sur-Lys that resulted in many men dead on both sides. It would have been worse had not the senior officers charged in to break it up, an act for which they were commended by Maximilian.

At first the king simply looked at the last disciplinary code and, after discussion with his commanders, made any necessary alterations, with no oath of obedience necessary from the soldiery. There is no code known for the expedition to Scotland in 1560. By the second quarter of the century company commanders were expected to swear in each man. Issuing such codes meant they could be tailored to the occasion. Leicester's code of 1585 for service in the Netherlands is one of the most imposing, beginning with a demand that every man receiving pay be bound by the articles. Discipline was usually the responsibility of the high marshal and provost marshal, and their greatest problem was desertion. Even hanging deserters as an example did not stop the rot. Matters were compounded by captains wanting leave; though the general or garrison commander would sign a pass for pressing matters at home, where no such need was apparent the captains simply went anyway. Shortage and irregularities in pay sparked off mutinies: in Ireland it was simmering almost non-stop. The mutiny in Ostend in 1588 even involved the gentlemen volunteers, and their grievances included ghastly victuals and bad quarters. They seized the governor, Sir John Conway, and despite royal sympathy Conway eventually brought in new troops and hanged one man from each of the nine companies involved.

Arguments and duels of honour marked out the men of rank. Two of Willoughby's colonels, Sir William Drury and Sir John Burgh, disagreed over precedence in the parade before King Henry. Two further arguments finally led to a duel in which Drury was seriously wounded in the arm. It was amputated and he died two days later.

THE KNIGHT IN BATTLE

In the early 16th century warfare was waged in much the same way as it had been in the previous century. When knights remained mounted they served as the shock troops of the army, using their heavy horses and lances to punch a hole through enemy ranks. However, light cavalry was also used for scouting and skirmishing, with a light spear that was not couched under the arm. The number of men of knightly rank should not be exaggerated. At Flodden in 1513 only one of the earl of Surrey's 500 retainers was a man-at-arms. The rest of the infantry was made up of missile troops, hedges of pikemen and billmen. Henry VIII insisted that men practise regularly with the bow but it was really a losing battle. Groups of handgunners were increasing in number, armed with either heavy muskets or lighter calivers.

In Audley's opinion, the bigger the army, the less shot (archers and handgunners) was required. These should be set around the other infantry three, four or five deep, two archers and two handgunners if four, but an extra archer if five. Having been harangued by the king and reminded of the plentiful coffers by the treasurer-at-war, the soldiers were roused by their captains, given food and drink and reminded that God was on their side. The council of war would presumably decide the order of battle: a square (the 'just square'), a rectangle (the 'broad rectangle') or more complex, such as the 'saw-tooth'. It is not certain how commands passed down the ranks but perhaps the sergeant was becoming a useful link in that chain of command. One formation placed wings of handgunners to filter the enemy on to the main body, as archers had done in the 14th century.

France

Supplying the army on campaign resulted in a number of clashes with varying outcomes. On 27 June 1513 the English supply train bound for the camp at Thérouanne, having reached Guines safely, set off under the eyes of Sir Edward Belknap and 300 men. It was joined by Sir Nicholas Vaux, captain of Guinne castle, with a further 24 horse and 36 foot. Near Ardres the cavalry stopped behind to drink and the infantry became more ragged, little-knowing a French force concealed in the woods was watching. Choosing their moment they fell on the hapless wagons; the carters cut the traces and fled on the

carthorses. The English cavalry made a hopeless effort but the archers used the cover of the wagons to hold off the enemy until their arrows ran out. Sir Nicholas failed in his attempt to rally the foot and both knights had to beat a retreat towards Guines, leaving many dead behind them, not to mention the entire supply train. Sir Rees ap Thomas set out from Thérouanne with his light horse but too late – the French had removed the wagons. Henry's commanders learned a bitter lesson: discipline was stepped up and numbers increased significantly, though attacks continued. The battle of the Spurs, however, (so-named from the fact that the French cavalry soon decided to quit the field, with the English horse in hot pursuit) resulted from a French attempt to resupply Thérouanne. Henry VIII (at this engagement surrounded by a bodyguard of mounted archers rather than gentlemen) took Maximilian's advice and placed light artillery pieces along a hill to guard the English mounted scouts. The English archers appear to have begun the French debacle but the cavalry sent them into full retreat. Cruickshank suggested that the panic might have been caused by a general fear of the English. The Venetian ambassador said of Shrewsbury that he came from the family of Talbot and to that day the French still threatened crying babies with the Talbots.

Scotland

In Scotland the English faced pikemen trained by French captains. Flodden in 1513 was the last major battle in Britain in which the longbow would take any great part. At Flodden the English cannon were hurried into position with commendable speed after marching round a bog. The damage done by the artillery on either side was not convincing, although it seems to have helped unsettle the Borderers and Huntly's Highlanders on the Scottish left, for they moved from their elevated position to launch the first charge. The English archers made some inroads on lightly armed Scots on the left and right of the line, but others were more heavily armoured and thus took fewer casualties. It

was the disciplined stand of the English columns that told most on the Scots, since the latter had always had a tendency to break if unsuccessful in the first rush. They were helped by the Scottish pikes, which might hold off horsemen but English billmen on foot hacked a way through by slicing the tops from the unwieldy pikes. Stanley's column may have displayed an early example of fire and movement – keeping enough troops to occupy the Highlanders' front while slipping the rest round to hit their flank. The battle of Pinkie Cleuch in 1547 has been called the first modern battle in Britain, since both sides used large numbers of pikemen and handgunners. The English also backed their army with an accompanying fleet, which bombarded the left of the Scots position from the Firth of Forth. Now archers, handgunners and artillery combined to stop and reverse the oncoming pike formations once the English cavalry had been repulsed. Spanish horse also galloped along and poured fire into their position. Such was the destruction that some 6,000 Scots were killed as opposed to 800 Englishmen. The victory allowed Somerset to establish garrisons in many places, but the cost of maintaining them was high and their presence alienated the natives. French pressure finally forced their abandonment in 1549. These defeats show that the disparate elements of the Scottish armies made cohesion difficult. Some, like the Highlanders and Borderers at

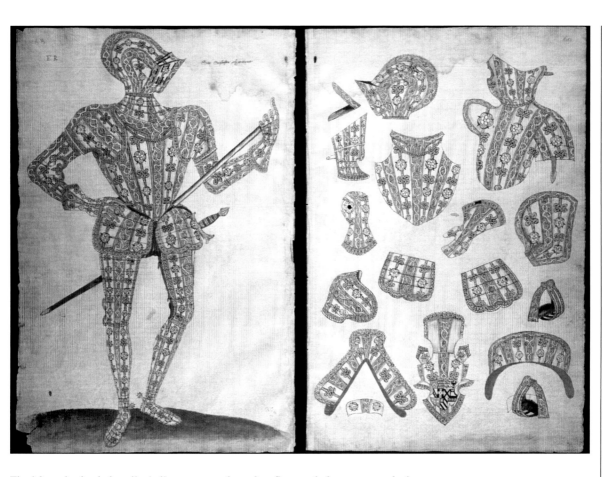

Flodden, lacked the discipline to stand under fire and threw away their advantage in a wild charge.

With so few of knightly rank present it may be thought there was little work for such people, but many knights still led from the front. At Flodden the flight of the Cheshire contingent left gaps that were exploited by the Scottish pikes, but knights such as Sir William FitzWilliam and Sir John Lawrence stood with their men and died to keep the enemy at bay. Edmund Howard was unhorsed twice or possibly more as he tried to reach his brother the Lord Admiral. Several knights were captured, including Sir Henry Grey. At Pinkie the English heavy horse and demi-lancers crashed into the Scottish pikes. Lord Arthur Grey of Wilton had led the cavalry and came out with a pike wound in the mouth and throat. Sir Andrew Flammach just managed to hold on to the royal standard, assisted by Sir Ralph Coppinger, a Gentleman Pensioner, although the snapped staff was seized by the Scots.

Religious conflict, ineptitude and rebellion

Religious unrest provided much of the exercise for English armies in the 16th century. Under Henry VIII this was largely due to the dissolution of the monasteries, which sparked the Pilgrimage of Grace in 1536–37. The 1549 southern revolts were a reaction to the spread of Protestantism, while in Elizabeth's reign the flight to England of Mary, Queen of Scots, saw the Northern Rebellion in 1569. Alarming as these were, the rebels lacked the calibre and the equipment of the men sent against them. In 1549 John Kett's

ABOVE **Armour for Sir Christopher Hatton, from the Jacob Album, which contains some 30 design drawings and is named after Jacob Halder, master armourer at Greenwich (1567–1607). This highly decorated garniture could be made up for the tilt using the reinforcing pieces seen on the right. On the left of this second page are a locking-gauntlet and matching pauldron, for the foot tourney; at the bottom are saddle steels and a demi-shaffron complete with coat-of-arms. (Victoria & Albert Museum)**

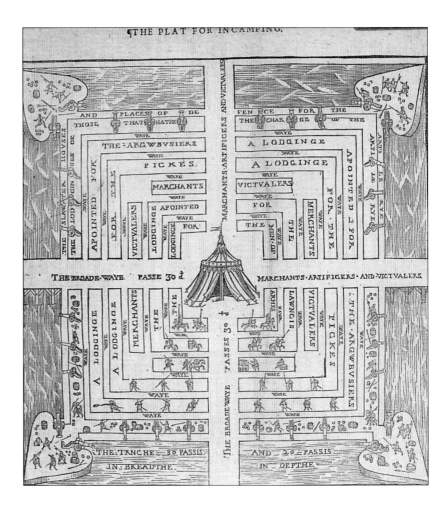

RIGHT **A camp, from Styward's _Parthwaie to Military Discipline_ of 1581. The higher the rank, the closer to the centre one was billeted. (Permission British Library)**

rebels were slaughtered at Dussindale by the earl of Warwick. The English nobility did not generally back the rebellions.

War in Elizabeth's reign was somewhat hampered by the Queen's natural tendency to hold back from committing her troops even after ordering an advance. This stemmed from her belief that battles could be lost and the consequences might then be infinitely worse. It stopped her commanders from being given free rein to capitalise on a promising situation. Elizabeth was not wholly to blame for lacklustre performance – indecision and bickering pervaded the entire hierarchy of command, while few of her generals showed any great aptitude in prosecuting war. One such episode took place during the invasion of Scotland in 1560, itself held up for three months, though the lapse was used to prop up the Scottish rebels and boost supplies for the English. At the siege of Leith, French forces came out and challenged the English during truce negotiations, but were successfully pushed back first by artillery and then by heavy horse. However, Lord Grey made no attempt to draw the whole force further out and cut off its retreat; only some French footsoldiers were accidentally caught out after chasing their enemies too far. The assault on the defences was worse: artillery failed to create wide enough breaches and flanking fire had not been dealt with adequately; all this occurred after Sir Ralph Saddler, Sir James Crofts and Kirkaldy of Grange had viewed the breach and advised Grey of the futility of an attack. To make matters worse, wall heights had been misjudged so that scaling ladders used against undamaged sections of wall were far too short. Grey blamed the duke of Norfolk, a lacklustre self-promoter, who readjusted the facts to clear himself, though both men were to blame. Grey had actually suggested at one point that Edinburgh was an easier target, though an attack would have jeopardised the regent and friendly Scots there.

In 1569 the earls of Northumberland and Westmorland raised a northern rebellion in favour of Mary, Queen of Scots. It was crushed when Lord Clinton and Robert Dudley, Earl of Leicester, marched to support the earl of Sussex in York. Lord Hunsdon quelled a smaller rebellion in 1570. The earl of Sussex invaded Scotland that year to chase the Borderers who had aided the Northern Rebellion and to back anti-French feeling.

Foreign assistance

In 1572, 300 volunteers crossed to the Low Countries, soon aided by Sir Humphrey Gilbert with 1,200 additional volunteer troops, to block Spanish occupation of the country. Further foreign adventures occurred, beginning in 1585 when the earl of Leicester was sent to the Netherlands to assist the Dutch against the Spanish. In 1589 Peregrine Bertie, Lord Willoughby, an able soldier who had proved his ability in the Netherlands, was sent to assist the Protestant Henry of Navarre to keep the French throne. The expedition should have been called off in late September when help was no longer required but Willoughby, with thoughts of honour in a glorious expedition, ignored the message from Sir Edward Stafford and set sail. Once in France the English troops joined those of Henry II of France and set out on 11 October; in 40 days and with full kit they marched 227 miles in cold, wet weather with muddy roads, little rest and sniping from French country folk who prevented attempts to leave in search of food. The suburbs of Paris fell but the king refused to seize the city itself for fear of damage and loss of good will; of 20 towns invested only four put up any resistance. Vendome fell to artillery fire that breached the walls. Le Mans fell to barrage, Willoughby ordering bridges of barrels lashed to ladders to take his men over the river on their side. At Alençon, Willoughby and his marshal made a special engine to pull down the drawbridge, enabling the fort to be seized, though their machine was lost the night before it could be employed on the town drawbridge. Although the King's troops were repulsed from the walls the garrison surrendered. The final stronghold, Falaise, was bombarded until two breaches were made, both so dangerous that a few enemy soldiers could hold them. Yet the French,

ABOVE **A rapier of about 1570–1600, found on the Thames foreshore together with a small by-knife, buckle and traces and leather belt. It is shown with a dagger found in the same area. (The Board of Trustees of the Armouries, XIX.1494)**

49

together with English officers and gentlemen (their main force being some miles away), seized them and opened the gates. A lone musketeer carried on firing until five cannon blasted his tower into the moat, from which he escaped, albeit a prisoner. The success for Henry was little owed to the English and Willoughby had lost more men from illness and hostile peasants than from battle. It is doubtful if the once-feared name of the English soldiery still had much impact.

The only real battle in which Elizabethan troops were involved took place at Nieuport, Holland, on 2 July 1600. Sir Francis Vere had brought over an English regiment to assist Prince Maurice of Nassau and acquitted himself well on 24 January 1598, when he pursued the Spanish invaders. Having ordered Dutch musketeers to keep up fire along the trees, he skirmished with the enemy squares. When the Prince's cavalry arrived Vere charged the rear of the squares while the Prince took the flanks. The Spanish musketeers fled and the allies got amongst the pikes. The Dutch cavalry chased after the retreating Spaniards but Vere held his horsemen to check the counterattack he knew would come. Sure enough, Spanish horse came after the Dutchmen but turned back when they saw Vere. In July 1600 a major clash occurred by the dunes near the sea, nine miles from Ostend. Vere held two ridges with his advanced guard to wear down the Spaniards but as things grew hot the reinforcements did not arrive and some 1,600 English troops found themselves holding back the whole Spanish army. Wounded twice in the leg, Vere encouraged his men but was forced to withdraw. When word finally reached the rear, counterattacks were launched that caught the tired Spaniards and broke them.

Three large naval and military expeditions also took place. In 1589 Sir Francis Drake and Sir John Norreys went to Portugal to annoy the Spanish and perhaps seize it back for the pretender Don Antonio. In 1596 the earl of Essex and Lord Howard (the lord admiral of Armada fame) landed at Cadiz. It was an opportunity to make large amounts from plunder, not just for the nobles (indeed, Essex and Howard mainly funded it with this reimbursement in mind) but also for the ordinary soldiers. The target was decided as Cadiz and Sir Francis Vere, the veteran commander in the Netherlands, withdrew 2,000 tried troops from there to provide experience in the force destined for Spain. Vere was desperate to go in first at dawn and even cut his cable when the anchor jammed in order to beat Sir Walter Raleigh. Essex and Vere landed to survey the beachhead before ordering in the first

BELOW **Peregrine Bertie, Lord Willoughby d'Eresby, resting in a Greenwich armour. A later copy. (The Board of Trustees of the Armouries, I.67)**

50

wave (of the better fighting men). Sir Conyers Clifford was sent to seize the narrow eastern peninsula and block Spanish help. A Spanish body attacked the assault force but retreated back, clambering over the rampart. This advertisement of entry was not lost and English troops followed and gained the wall top. Essex then joined them, to be confronted by a 20ft drop, but luckily Vere had sent men round to find and force a gate, which they did. The message being lost he charged the main gates with his main force and broke in. Essex, having arrived by this less precipitous route, then impetuously charged into the market place with only 30 or so men, but luck and the methodical Vere who called in his own soldiers as he advanced was then able to scatter opposition and join up with Essex and capture the town and castle within a day.

Conflict in Ireland

In Ireland the English experience differed from that in mainland Europe. English troops stationed there from Elizabeth's early reign faced Shane O'Neill's uprising in 1567 and the Desmond War of 1579–81. At first Irish soldiers were equipped with close-combat weapons together with bows and javelins. However, later in the century Hugh O'Neill, Earl of Tyrone, had welded together a force equipped with muskets and calivers and including many men trained in Spain; not only were the Irish well drilled in pikes and musketry but they used the boggy, woody terrain to advantage. In 1594 the Nine Years War broke out and the tactics were put to good use. At the Ford of the Biscuits near Enniskillen the English were defeated, as they were next year at Clontibret and Curlew Hills. In 1598 O'Neill ambushed another English force on the march at Yellow Ford and caused heavy casualties by both musketry and close combat. Provoked, the earl of Essex arrived with another army in 1599, but

BELOW **A woodcut from Derricke's *Image of Ireland* shows an English force with demi-lancers in three-quarter armour, pikemen and caliver men. (Permission British Library)**

O'Neill had the good sense to bide his time and wait. Next year Essex was replaced by Lord Mountjoy, who thought brutality was an effective weapon. He also tried to pen the cattle and so starve the Irish rebels but his move on Ulster on 2 October 1600 was defeated at Moyry Pass by fire from O'Neill's musketeers protected behind field fortifications. Mountjoy moved to confront a Spanish force of 3,500 men that landed at Kinsale in September 1601 and, weakened by sickness, would have fared badly if O'Neill's relief force had blockaded him when it arrived. However, although not in the kind of terrain that suited Celtic fighting, O'Neill decided to take the offensive. He bungled a night march against the English camp and Mountjoy reacted swiftly. The cavalry chased the Irish horse from the field while the Irish infantry, ordered into Spanish squares by O'Neill, could not cope efficiently. O'Neill's change to the tactical defensive, as opposed to the strategic defence of Ulster and the tactical offensive, had been more than his men could achieve; one defeat had broken the spell of O'Neill's victories. Two years later he surrendered. This folly, together with poor command structure, had come up against a powerful royal army backed by naval support.

BELIEF AND BELONGING – CHIVALRY

The code of chivalry was still alive. Fighting for honour and for the good, to protect women and the poor, had always been an ethos that some knights aspired to and others ignored. Battlefields were now largely the preserve of professional soldiers, with even less room for knights to display chivalry, partly because there were fewer knights involved in active warfare. In the Middle Ages no self-respecting knight used a bow or crossbow in battle as a matter of course; by the later 16th century Sir John Smythe was being depicted in the Jacob Album with pistol in hand, hardly a weapon for close combat. Those men of the rank of knight still felt part of an elite group but it included many ranks of society, from the king down through his dukes and earls to lesser landowners and men from mercantile backgrounds who had done good service. Wealth and position in society no longer devolved purely from landholding. Knights were at first still made by other knights, such as when Charles Brandon dubbed John Dudley in 1523 for his valour at the crossing of the Somme. But knights finally lost this right during the reign of Elizabeth, when all applications had to be passed to the Privy Council for vetting.

BELOW **Armour for Sir John Smythe, about 1585. Made at Augsburg but with additions at Greenwich. This is a light cavalry armour with pieces of exchange for an officer of infantry's armour. The burgonet helmet has a falling buffe. A wheellock pistol is carried. (The Board of Trustees of the Armouries, II.84, III.1430-1, XII.716)**

The panoply of chivalry continued in its most sensationalist form at the meeting of Henry VIII and Francis I of France at the celebrated Field of Cloth of Gold near Calais, in 1520. Lavish banquets, fountains of wine, tournaments, archery and even wrestling between the two kings made a magnificent pageant that attempted to offer the idea of friendship. Chivalry could also be seen in the field – in 1589 the earl of Essex rammed his pike into the gates of Lisbon to offer single combat on behalf of his mistress. Bravado could be lethal, however – at Zutphen in 1586, Sir Philip Sidney's decision to follow the new thinking and leave off limb defences resulted in his death. Sir John Smythe felt that, had Sidney worn his cuisses, the musket ball would have been sufficiently slowed down and not broken his thighbone.

Royal prisoners, dukes, lieutenants general, great constables etc. belonged to Henry and it was a capital offence for anyone else to hold them for ransom or free them. They must be taken to the king or commander immediately in return for a reward. The notion of chivalric behaviour survived most noticeably in siege warfare. A herald would formally demand surrender and, if refused, would appear once more before the siege began in earnest. The garrison at Thérouanne was allowed to march out (23 August 1513) although this could have been also because of their strong position. Jousts between six gentlemen on both sides were run under the walls of Thérouanne in 1534, on the invitation of Sir John Wallop whose troops were moving through the area destroying the countryside.

William Caxton had printed Raimon Llull's *The Book of the Ordre of Chyvalry or Knyghthode* in about 1484, and in 1485 printed Sir Thomas Malory's eight romances under the title *Le Morte d'Arthur*. In 1523 John Bourchier, Lord Berners, under the command of Henry VIII himself, translated the works of Froissart with a similar aim: to inspire valiant deeds. These books gave the hope that chivalry could be revived as it had once been; indeed such medieval works managed in England to survive the Renaissance, even though its classical leanings spelled the end of chivalric literature across the Channel in France. Already in a newly Protestant England Roger Ascham in *The Scholemaster* regretted the day when Mallory's work was read in the court at the expense of the Bible, and linked the Middle Ages with Catholicism, when chivalric works came from idle monks and wanton canons. By the time Edmund

RIGHT **Robert Radcliffe, Earl of Sussex, *c.*1590, wearing armour for foot combat over the barrier. The right pauldron is not cut away for a lance and there is no lance-rest. Leg-armour is discarded since blows below the barrier are forbidden. Note the elaborate helmet plume. He holds a pike, while his sword scabbard has the side-piece attached to the broad hanger, which in turn has been unhooked from its ring at his belt. (The Board of Trustees of the Armouries, I.36)**

Spenser published his *Faerie Queene* (1590–96) chivalry was a reminder of 'antique times', now becoming a memory. In Spain, Cervantes' *Don Quixote* of 1605 was the greatest literary knock to the ideals of chivalry, which would also soon disappear from 17th-century Puritan England, until revived in the 19th century.

MUSEUMS

The major collection of 16th-century armour in the United Kingdom is housed in the Royal Armouries. Its museum in Leeds holds a number of Greenwich armours including both the 1520 armours of Henry VIII, as well as many from European centres for comparison, together with all types of weapons. The Royal Armouries' museum in the Tower of London has the earliest Greenwich armour, made for Henry VIII, together with his 1540 garniture. There are also other Greenwich items. Many of the munition armour pieces, as well as weapons of the king's guard, can also be seen. Also in London, the Wallace Collection has some good pieces and the Victoria and Albert Museum a few important items. The other surviving armour of Henry VIII in Britain resides at Windsor Castle. Kelvingrove in Glasgow has the well-preserved armour of the earl of Pembroke.

In the United States the Metropolitan Museum in New York houses the 1527 armour for Henry VIII. It also has the best-preserved Greenwich garniture, that of the earl of Cumberland, plus other Greenwich armours.

GLOSSARY

Aiglet	Metal tip fixed to a point to allow it to pass through an eyelet.
Anime	Cuirass made from several horizontal lames.
Armet	Closed helmet that opens at each side to be put on.
Arming doublet	Lightly padded doublet worn beneath armour, with mail gussets or sleeves and with arming points attached.
Arming partlet	Quilted collar worn below a plate collar.
Arquebus	Longarm, usually a matchlock of varying bore.
Backplate	Defence for the back of the torso.
Baldric	Belt worn diagonally across the shoulder.
Bard	Full plate armour for a horse.
Base	Skirt, either of cloth or steel.
Basinet	Conical or globular open-faced helmet that extended down at the sides and back.
Bevor	Defence for the lower face and chin.
Boar-spear	Broad-bladed spear with two lugs below the blade to prevent a boar running up the shaft.
Bodkin	An instrument for pricking.
Breastplate	Defence for the front of the torso.
Brigandine	Armour consisting of a canvas jacket inside which is riveted by many small plates.

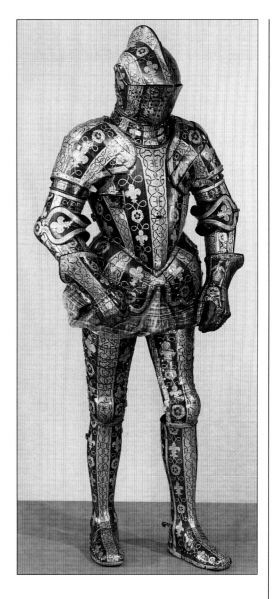

ABOVE **Armour garniture of George Clifford, third Earl of Cumberland. This is the best surviving Greenwich garniture, made in 1590 at Greenwich. (All rights reserved, The Metropolitan Museum of Art, 32.130.6a–y)**

Burgonet	Open helmet with neck-defence, peak and cheek-pieces.
Buskins	Boots made from soft leather or velvet.
By-knife	Small knife carried in a scabbard or dagger-sheath.
Caliver	Longarm of medium-regular bore.
Canions	Cloth extension down the thigh.
Cannon	Plate defence for the upper or lower arm.
Cantle	Rear part of a saddle.
Chape	The metal reinforce at the tip of a scabbard.
Close-helmet	Helmet covering the head that opens by pivoting the front and back halves.
Codpiece	Plate defence for the genitals. Also a similar cloth covering for civilian wear.
Coronel	Ring of points attached to a lance for the jousts of peace.
Couter	Plate defence for the elbow.
Cranequin	Spanning device for crossbows consisting of a ratchet and winder.
Crinet	Plate defence for a horse's neck.
Crupper	Plate defence for a horse's rump.
Cuirass	Defence for the torso.
Cuisse	Plate defence for the thigh.
Culet	Plate defence below the back-plate.
Estoc	Pointed thrusting sword.
Falling-buffe	Defence for the lower face, made from lames that can be lowered over one another.
Fauld	Hooped skirt attached to the lower edge of the cuirass.
Flanchard	Plate defence for a horse's flank.
Fuller	Groove running down a sword blade to lighten it.
Gauntlet	Defence for the hand and wrist.
Gorget	Collar.
Grandguard	Reinforce worn over the shoulder and upper chest in jousts.
Graper	Spiked ring attached to a lance behind the hand that butts against the lance-rest.
Greave	Defence for the lower leg.
Halberd	Staff weapon consisting of an axe blade backed by a hook and topped by a spike.
Hanger	Wide, shield-shaped sling to carry the scabbard.
Haute-piece	Upstanding plate on the pauldron.
Helm	Helmet with protruding lower lip, for use in jousts.
Impresa	Decorative tournament shield designed for display only.
Jack of plate	Defence for ordinary soldiers consisting of a jacket enclosing small plates secured by twine.
Jousts	Contest between two mounted opponents with lances.
Jousts of peace	Jousts in which blunt weapons are used.
Jousts of war	Jousts in which sharp weapons are used.
Lame	Strip or plate of steel, sometimes used to provide articulation in armour.
Lance-rest	Bracket attached to the breastplate to prevent a lance running back through the armpit when a strike is made.
Left-hand gauntlet	Gauntlet, often of mail, used to grasp an opponent's blade.
Lists	The arena in a tournament.
Locket	The metal mount at the mouth of a scabbard.
Locking-gauntlet	Gauntlet for the right hand that can be secured in the closed position to prevent loss of a weapon in the tourney.
Manifer	Reinforce worn over the gauntlet and lower arm defences in the jousts.
Matchlock	A gun fired by lowering a glowing slow match onto gunpowder.
Morion	An open helmet with high comb, wide brim and cheek-pieces.
Morris pike	A pike, probably a corruption of 'Moorish pike'.
Musket	A heavy longarm usually fired from a rest.
Pantoffles	Leather overshoes; also cloth slippers.
Partisan	Staff weapon consisting of a long tapering blade furnished with two flukes at its base.
Pasguard	Reinforce worn over the couter in jousts.
Pauldron	Plate defence for the shoulder.
Peascod	Fashionable style of drawn-down waist for doublet or breastplate.
Petronel	Longarm with shortened barrel and curved stock to fire from chest, for use on horseback.

Peytral	Chest defence for a horse.
Pickadils	Leather or fabric tabs decorating the main edges of pieces of armour.
Pieces of advantage	Reinforces worn during certain tournament events.
Plackart	Plate stomach defence.
Point	Twine or leather strip used to fasten clothing or armour.
Poleyn	Plate defence for the knee.
Pollaxe	Staff weapon consisting of an axe blade backed by a hammer and topped by a spike. Some have a hammer backed by a spike.
Pommel	The piece on the end of a sword hilt to counterbalance the blade. Also the front board of a saddle.
Quintain	Dummy used for weapon practice.
Rapier	Long, narrow-bladed thrusting sword with elaborate hilt.
Ricasso	The blunt portion of a sword blade beyond the hilt to allow a finger to be hooked over it.
Sabaton	Defence for the foot.
Sallet	Helmet drawn out to a tail at the rear.
Scallops	Decorative edging made by slitting.
Shaffron	Defence for a horse's head.
Side-piece	The diagonal strap attaching the scabbard to the front of the belt.
Skull	The main part of a helmet; also a simple steel cap.
Slow match	Length of cord soaked in saltpetre.
Snaphance	Gun in which ignition is caused by sparks from a flint striking a steel.
Sneck hook	Small pivoting hook for securing through a pierced stud.
Spanish morion	Open helmet with tall skull, wide brim and cheek pieces.
Upper and lower stocks	The hose divided into two parts.
Targe	Circular shield carried on foot.
Tasset	Plate defence for the thigh, attached to the fauld.
Tilt	Barrier down the centre of the lists; also the term for jousts over the barrier.
Tilt visor	Visor with very narrow sights, used in the jousts over a barrier.
Tonlet	Deep laminated plate skirt.
Touch box	Container for carrying priming powder for a firearm.
Tournament	Military event in which various contests take place.
Tourney	The team event in a tournament.
Trousse	Set of hunting implements.
Tuck	English thrusting sword.
Turner	The upper part of an upper cannon, which turns independently to aid arm movement.
Two-hand sword	Large sword designed for use in both hands.
Vambrace	Plate defence for the arm.
Venetians	Trunks fastening below the knee.
Ventail	Defence for the mouth and throat.
Volant-piece	Brow reinforce.
War hammer	Hammer backed by a beak, for use on horseback.
Wheellock	Gun in which ignition is caused by sparks from iron pyrites pressed against a spinning abrasive wheel.
Wrapper	A reinforce for the bevor.

BIBLIOGRAPHY

Blair, Claude, *European Armour*, B.T. Batsford Ltd, London, 1958

Boynton, L., *The Elizabethan Militia 1558–1638*, Routledge & Kegan Paul, London, 1967

Cornish, Paul, *Henry VIII's Army*, Osprey Publishing Ltd, London, 1987

Cruickshank, G.C., *Elizabeth's Army*, (2nd ed.), Oxford University Press, London, 1966

Cruickshank, G.C., *Army Royal*, Oxford University Press, London, 1969

Dillon, The Viscount, 'Tilting in Tudor Times', *Archaeological Journal*, 1898

Eaves, Ian, 'On the Remains of a Jack of Plate Excavated from Beeston Castle in Cheshire', *The Journal of the Arms & Armour Society*, vol. XIII, 2, Sept, 1989

Eaves, Ian, 'The Tournament Armours of King Henry VIII of England', *Livrustkammaren* 1993, Stockholm, 1994

Eaves, Ian, 'The Greenwich Armour and Locking-Gauntlet of Sir Henry Lee in the Collection of the Worshipful Company of Armourers and Brasiers', *The Journal of the Arms & Armour Society*, vol. XVI, 3 Sept, 1999

Ferguson, Arthur B., 'The Indian Summer of English Chivalry', *Studies in the Decline and Transformation of Chivalric Idealism*, Durham, N.C., 1960

Gruffudd, Elis, 'Suffolk's expedition to Montdidier', 1523, trans. M.B. Davies, *Bulletin of the Faculty of Arts, Fouad I University*, vol. vii, 1944

Gruffudd, Elis, 'The enterprises of Paris and Boulogne', trans. M.B. Davies, *Bulletin of the Faculty of Arts, Fouad I University*, vol. xi, 1949

Gruffudd, Elis, 'Boulogne and Calais from 1545 to 1550', trans. M.B. Davies, *Bulletin of the Faculty of Arts, Fouad I University*, vol. xii, 1950

Hooker, J.R., 'The organization and supply of the Tudor military under Henry VII', *Huntington Library Quarterly*, vol. 23

Kelly, Francis M. and Schwabe, Randolph, *A Short History of Costume and Armour, 1066–1800*, David & Charles Reprints, Newton Abbot, 1972

Norman, A.V.B. and Pottinger, Don, *Warrior to Soldier 449–1660*, Weidenfeld & Nicolson Ltd, London, 1966

Norman, A.V.B., *The Rapier and Small Sword, 1460–1820*, Arms and Armour Press, London, 1980

Norris, Herbert, *Tudor Costume and Fashion*, Dover Publications, 1997

Oman, Sir Charles, *A History of the Art of War in the Sixteenth Century*, London, 1937

Phyrr, Stuart W., La Rocca, Donald J. and Breiding, Dirk H., The *Armored Horse in Europe, 1480–1620*, Metropolitan Museum of Art, New York, 2005

Sutcliffe, Matthew, *The practice, proceedings and lawes of armes*, London, 1593

Tincey, John, *The Armada Campaign 1588*, Osprey Publishing Ltd, London, 1988

Watts, Karen, 'Henry VIII and the Pageantry of the Tudor Tournament', *Livrustkammaren*, 1994

Williams, Alan and Reuck, Anthony de, *The Royal Armoury at Greenwich 1515–1649 – A History of its Technology*, Royal Armouries Monographs, London, 1995

Young, Alan, *Tudor and Jacobean Tournaments*, George Philip, London, 1987

One of the first decorated English snaphance pistols, c.1600. The walnut stock is inlaid with engraved bone and mother-of-pearl, the metal damascened with gold. It being only a foot long, Holinshed called this type 'a pretty short snapper'. (The Board of Trustees of the Armouries, XII.1823)

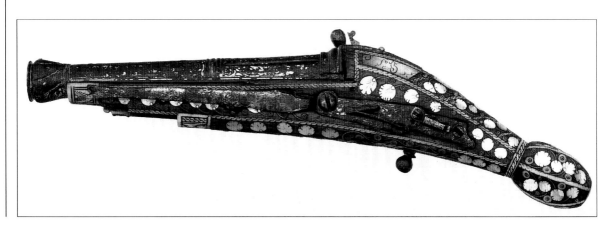

COLOUR PLATE COMMENTARY

A: KNIGHT, C.1525

This knight of about 1525 **(1)** is based on the so-called Genouilhac armour in the Metropolitan Museum of Art, New York, probably that made for Henry VIII in 1527 at Greenwich and the earliest surviving English garniture, consisting of a number of pieces that could be made up for field or tournament use. The lance-rest is adjusted by a screw. The close-helmet **(2)** comprises a visor, upper bevor and lower bevor, all pivoting from a single point each side of the skull. The helmet rotates on a flanged collar, secured by a sprung, pierced stud on the front edge of the skull that locates a hole in the lower bevor and is secured by a small hook. The disc at the rear may have helped keep the strap of a wrapper in

place. The interior was fitted with a padded lining stitched to internal leather bands riveted in place. **(3)** Interior of the unique three-part breastplate. **(4)** Instead of having a large plate with smaller lames above and below, Greenwich pauldrons were composed of equal-sized lames overlapping upwards. Internally these were held on five or (as here) six sets of leathers rather than with sliding rivets at the outer side. Haute-pieces (to deflect lateral blows) on the pauldrons of Greenwich armours can be seen as late as 1585 and were always detachable. The vambrace was attached by a point from the arming doublet through a leather tab. The couter wing attached via a pivot hook. The sabaton **(5)** closed via a pierced stud and pivot hook. The rowel spur arms slid through slots and a pin secured it at the rear through a pierced stud. The tilt reinforces **(6)** are based on Henry VIII's 1540 garniture and comprise a grandguard over the chest, pasguard at the elbow and manifer over the forearm and hand. A hole in the manifer fits over a pierced stud on the gauntlet and is secured by a hook; the disc protects it. **(7)** Locking gauntlet or 'close-gauntlet' for the tourney: the 'fingers' closed over and were secured by a pivot-hook, preventing loss of a weapon. **(8)** A type of close-helmet (like similar armets) found in English churches c.1500–40, with 'sparrow's beak' visor. Some later examples had gorget plates. A reinforcing plate riveted to the front or left of the bevor. Sword with finger-guards **(9)**, possibly North Italian, c.1520. A long-sleeved shirt **(10)** of linen or other fine stuff was worn next to the skin, often embroidered. At the start of the century it was low-necked but slowly rose to a high neck. A padded doublet **(11)** was worn over the shirt, over which came the jerkin (jacket), some so similar they are difficult to distinguish, but others had a deep 'V'- or 'U'-shaped opening reaching the waist. The jerkin had a skirt reaching the knees, those with tubular pleats being known as 'bases'. Long hose of shaped cloth were tied to the doublet by twine or silk points tipped with metal aiglets. The upper part (upper stocks) was sometimes slashed and puffed and after 1515 was made fuller. The stockings (nether stocks) were stitched on anywhere from the knee to below the seat. Broad and square-toed shoes and boots were often slashed. Open-fronted shoes were fastened by a strap around the instep. Boots were either close-fitted and laced, or loose and knee-length.

B: THE BATTLE OF THE SPURS, 16 AUGUST 1513

The army of Henry VIII was besieging the French town of Thérouanne when a French force hoping to relieve it found itself facing the main English army. Rebuffed by artillery, it then found the English heavy horse bearing down on it, and decided the best course lay in a fast retreat across the fields near Guingate, thus giving the battle its name. It was asserted that this was a ploy to lure the English into a trap but no ambush was forthcoming. The knights of both sides wear

LEFT **Greenwich armour of Lord Buckhurst, c.1590. This armour is fitted with a burgonet with vertical bars. (Reproduced by kind permission of the trustees of the Wallace Collection, London)**

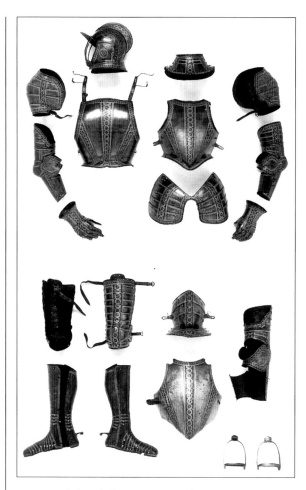

armets and close-helmets and colourful cloth bases around their waists. In this period decorative horse caparisons often concealed steel armour.

C: FIELD MEDICINE, 1522

In 1522 John Russell, gentleman, landed with an English raiding party on the coast of Brittany and attacked the town of Morlaix. A culverin shattered the gate and the English made a rush that broke through into the streets beyond. During the attack John was wounded by an arrow and lost the sight in his right eye. However the town was captured and, on returning to his ship, he and several others were knighted by the Admiral, Sir John Howard. Sir John Russell would subsequently become first Earl of Bedford in 1555 under instructions left in the will of Henry VIII, for services to the crown.

John wears an arming doublet, lightly padded and with mail gussets to cover gaps in the plates at the elbow and armpit. Arming points are used to tie through leather tabs or holes in the plates to secure pauldrons, vambraces and cuisses.

If barbed arrowheads were used they had to be flattened with pincers before extraction. If deeply embedded in a wound the head might be pushed right out the other end and snapped off. Gunshot wounds were probed to locate a ball before slender pincers were inserted to grasp it; tatters of clothing also had to be removed. Bullets were thought to poison a wound, and so it was cleansed by pouring boiling elder oil into it. This caused terrible pain and often resulted in fever and inflammation. The great French surgeon, Ambroise Paré, ran out of oil on one occasion and instead resorted to the old method of egg yolk and turpentine; he discovered this had far better effects, but his methods were slow to catch on everywhere. Boiling oil seems sometimes to have been used to cleanse other wounds as well. Cannonballs and bullets could smash a bone, so amputation was a general answer. The operation might be swift, with screws used to compress blood vessels above the site of the operation, but there was little knowledge of cleanliness and none of bacteria. In order to remove a leg, the patient might sit on a chair with the limb laid on a bench. A surgeon's assistant might hold the patient from behind while another sat astride the leg to hold it above the site of operation; a third held the lower part of the limb up slightly clear of the bench. Where possible, broken limbs could be set between wooden splints. Dislocations were treated in much the same way as today. Pain might be numbed by pressing the nerve in the neck, administering poppy juice or even giving a strong drink of liquor.

D: KNIGHT, C.1550

Garnitures varied in their composition and some were designed purely for the field. This figure (1) is based on the Greenwich armour of Henry Herbert, Earl of Pembroke, in the Kelvingrove Museum, Glasgow. A form of cuirass that is sometimes seen from the 1530s to about 1560 is the anime. Instead of being made from a single large piece, a number of horizontal-shaped lames are riveted together; smaller individual plates made it easier to control the thickness and strength of the metal during manufacture – something more difficult to achieve with a large sheet of steel. A close-burgonet is fitted with a falling-buffe. Mail sabatons with steel toecaps remained popular until c.1570. The horse's shaffron, peytral, crupper and saddle steels are made to match. Additional pieces (2) allow other armours to be built: a reinforcing breastplate can be added to the heavy field armour to help absorb the impact of bullets from increasingly efficient gunpowder weapons. For a medium field armour the lance-rest and lower leg defences were left off; for a light field armour an open burgonet was worn whilst the arm defences were replaced by mail sleeves (or perhaps elbow-length defences and long-cuffed gauntlets) and the upper leg defences were removed. An officer of foot was similar to the light field but might include the arm defences, while tasset extensions were added via keyhole slots engaging with turning pins in the lower lames of the tassets. (3)

hawks. The most dangerous animal was the wild boar, at the time increasingly rare in England and destined to become extinct during the 17th century. Large mastiffs or alaunts were used to seize the animal by the ears. It could be attacked with a boar-spear furnished with a lug either side of the blade socket to prevent the animal running up the shaft; boar-swords (rare in England) similarly had blades with a bar fitted through a slot near the point. Deer were hunted with greyhounds in couples, or deerhounds. Breaking (cutting up) a deer was a skill and men of good birth would be taught how to dismember a kill as part of their training. Rarely, a trousse might be carried, a kit containing a knife with a cleaver-like blade and various eviscerating implements in slits in the sheath.

For the fashionably dressed, large cartwheel ruffs of the period from 1580 comprised several layers. Made from starched linen, lace, cambric or lawn, rain made them floppy 'like the disclout of a slut' according to Stubbes. Ruffs were now mirrored by hand ruffs. Many preferred the falling band, a collar attached to the shirt and turned down over that of the doublet. Funnel-shaped turned-back cuffs were made to match. The padded 'peascod' doublet was fashionable from about 1575 to 1590, while tight sleeves were supplemented by fuller versions, or the bishop sleeve and trunk sleeve (leg-of-mutton style). The unpadded jerkin often had a longer skirt, otherwise remaining similar to the doublet. Ceremonial or dressing gowns continued. Short cloaks were joined by ankle-length versions in the 1570s, or those with hoods, sleeves or shoulder capes.

By the 1570s the onion-shaped breeches began to be superseded by a style that swelled before turning in sharply at the bottom. The codpiece now shrank and was rare by 1590. The left-hand figure with the wheellock wears Venetians (popular from 1570), fastened below the knee, either close-fitting or padded out and lacking a codpiece. His companion with the hunting crossbow wears extensions down the thigh called canions; both types were still trussed to the doublet. From about 1570 fine stockings worn under boots might be protected by thick boot-hose, which soon became more ornate and were worn with shoes. Until 1585 boots were usually worn only for riding. As well as patterns, pantoffles were worn as leather overshoes with cork soles, or soft ones as indoor slippers. By 1600 a wedge-shaped heel appeared for the first time.

The flat cap worn at an angle had been relegated by 1570, but other styles of bonnet were worn (usually of silk or velvet). One had a small crown gathered into a band (known as a court bonnet), another had a tam-o'-shanter style of crown and one had a tall bag-shaped crown and slight brim. Hats (usually of felt but also beaver for the rich after 1575) appeared again, especially one with a sugar-loaf crown.

Colours were seen to reflect a person's state of mind and symbolism was also reflected in the embroidery pattern and choice of flowers. The Queen liked white and black as symbolising virginity and many of her more flattering courtiers also chose these colours.

Matching burgonet. **(4)** A close burgonet, made at Greenwich c.1555. **(5)** and **(6)** swords, c.1540. **(7)** War hammer, c.1560. **(8)** A wheellock petronel, the butt designed to be held against the chest rather than the shoulder. Robert Dudley proudly holds one in a portrait. The doublet **(9)** began to be pointed down at the front, the padded rolls on the shoulder now being common. The jerkin also had padded rolls (wings) and the short-sleeved style shown here was popular. The long gown was now relegated to ceremonial wear but simpler versions were worn in private life. Proper trunk hose now appeared (usually slashed), no longer referred to as 'upper stocks'. The shape was achieved by padding out with 'bombast', e.g. horsehair, wool or bran. Stockings might now be knitted for the first time. The feathered cap, enhanced by jewels and brooches, was very popular.

E: ELIZABETHAN HUNTING SCENE

Hunts were good exercise and provided extra meat. They might be carefully planned to drive the game down to where the huntsmen were waiting, armed with crossbows, bows or wheellocks. Small crossbows were sometimes carried in the saddle; the cord could be drawn back by a cranequin (the handle cranking a ratchet that engaged teeth on the drawing bar to wind it back) or a goat's-foot lever. Crossbows were sometimes even combined with a wheellock. Some small game was killed by blunt heads that prevented the bolt penetrating and literally blowing it apart, although many preferred to hunt birds and small game with falcons and

F: A GREENWICH GARNITURE, C.1580

Based on the blued and gilt Greenwich garniture of the third earl of Cumberland in the Metropolitan Museum of Art, New York (also shown in the Jacob Album), the main figure **(1)** wears the armour made up for field use as a heavy cavalryman. The cuirass is connected together at the sides by pins securing hinged hasps to pierced studs (usual except for several late armours that have shoulder straps and buckles, and a belt riveted to the back plate). Greenwich cuirasses tend to be flat and until about 1585 to overlap one or more waist-lames. A style of gauntlet emerged in which the metacarpal plate extends to guard the base of the thumb and the cuff similarly extends on the inner side under the thumb. The cuff is hinged until very late in the century. Greenwich pauldrons have a 'humpy look', often with a 'blister' near the collarbone covering the pierced lug and pin of the shoulder hasp that connects the breast- and backplates. By the later 16th century laminated cuisses were popular, as here. For heavy field use a reinforcing breastplate was sometimes added, together with a wrapper worn over the upper bevor. **(2)** Close-helmet with field visor; the front and rear are closed by a stud and keyhold slot on the gorget plates. In England additional pieces **(3)** for the tournament were known as 'double pieces', 'pieces of advantage' or 'pieces of exchange'. Pieces for the tilt include the tilt visor with narrow, low-vision slits. The lower edge of the armet closes over a flanged edge on the collar and locks via a pivot hook at the chin. The visor fits into the upper bevor; some have a long pivot hook that clamps over the lifting peg to prevent the visor being flung up if struck. The hook is held in this position by a sprung stud pressing against it. **(4)** Grandguard; the hasp on the right attaches on the wearer's left side of the helmet, while the hole on the left of the face-guard fits over the pierced lug on the upper bevor and secures with a split pin. Slots on the chest fit over a staple. The pasguard **(5)** is secured to the elbow by a split pin through a pierced lug on the couter below. A strap on the grandguard secures the upper half. The manifer **(6)** straps over the gauntlet, while a strap from the pasguard is buckled through a slot in the cuff. For the tourney a reinforcing breast, wrapper and also a visor reinforce and a locking gauntlet might be worn. For the foot tournament the field armour was given a right pauldron that mirrored the left one rather than being cut away for a lance-rest; leg-armour was removed and a wrapper fitted. **(7)** One of four matching vamplates for lances. Demi-shaffron **(8)** to protect the upper part of the horse's head over the tilt barrier. Matching saddle steels **(9)**; en suite stirrups were also provided. **(10)** Cuisse, poleyn, greave and sabaton of a contemporary armour for Sir Henry Lee. The laminated strips around the ankle are a feature of some Greenwich armours. The spur is a fixture. **(11)** The pauldron was usually attached via a hole to a stud on the collar or on the shoulder hasp; the stud either had a spring-loaded barb to stop the pauldron slipping over the end, as here, or was pierced for a split pin. The turner **(12)** was a short piece fitted at the top of the vambrace, whose grooved lower edge enclosed the flanged upper edge of the upper cannon, allowing the two to rotate independently. **(13)** Lug on rear plate of greave secured through a hole on the front plate by the springiness of the steel itself. **(14)** Pivot hook through pierced lug on lower cannon. **(15)** Keyhole slot and domed rivet. **(16)** Keyhole slot and turning pin.

G: THE ACCESSION DAY TILTS, C.1586

The Accession Day tilts took place fairly regularly on 17 November, the date that Elizabeth ascended the throne. They were usually held at Whitehall tiltyard, which ran north–south instead of east–west, with the royal gallery at one end facing north rather than in the middle where the clash would occur. Here Sir Henry Lee, Queen's Champion at the Tilt, tries to shatter his blunted and hollow lance against his opponent to score points. The tilt was actually the wooden barrier separating the contestants. Lee may have entered the arena with an impresa, which would be presented by his page. This was a flimsy tournament display shield, painted with a theme and probably a suitable motto; by the late 1570s these seem to have replaced coats-of-arms in the lists. Lee wears a partially etched and gilt Greenwich garniture of the time, with narrow tilt visor and tilt reinforces – grandguard, pasguard and manifer – in place. Anyone wishing to hold a tournament had to petition the monarch and by the early 16th century this could be in fantasy terms, such as from 'Lady May' in 1506 to Princess Mary. Challenges were also of this form: in 1581 the 'Four Foster Children of Desire' (Sidney and three other nobles) challenged the Queen to give up the Fortress of Beauty or send her knights against them. Such literary challenges might well be verbally answered by an opponent before combat even started. Moreover, contestants were keen to spout a literary piece (not always written personally) when making their entrance into the arena.

H: KNIGHT, C.1590

This figure (1) is wearing a three-quarter Greenwich armour based on that of Sir James Scudamore in the Metropolitan Museum of Art, New York. It is fitted with a burgonet and falling-buffe, the latter lowered to allow air to the face This is a medium field armour, the type worn by a demi-lance; the lighter lance carried meant that no lance-rest was needed. Burgonet with falling-buffe (2), from a Greenwich armour of Sir Henry Lee. The buffe slots over a rectangular lug each side of the burgonet and is secured by the hook on the hasp fitting through a pierced lug on the burgonet. (3) Burgonet of Lord Buckhurst fitted with face grille, c.1590. (4) Target, from the design for an armour for Sir Henry Lee. Targets were inspired by Spanish shields and were sometimes carried before an officer. In battle they could be used to deflect pikeheads. (5) Rapier, probably English, c.1600, the hilt encrusted with silver. The scabbard is fitted to receive a by-knife and a bodkin, the latter perhaps for piercing eyelets for points. (6) Left-hand dagger, probably English, c.1600. (7) Fencing with sword and dagger. The figure wears a doublet of fence and full trunk hose. (8) Wheellock pistol, late 16th century. This uses the spinning action of an abrasive wheel against a piece of iron pyrites to create sparks and so touch off the powder in the priming pan, which then flashes through a hole into the barrel to ignite the main charge. A spanner winds up the wheel, whose axle in turning winds a small chain round it that connects to a now-tensed spring. Pressing the trigger releases the spring that pulls on the chain, so unwinding it and spinning the wheel. The iron pyrites is held in the jaws of a pivoting cock that rests on top of a pan cover. As the wheel spins, a cam swings the pan cover open to reveal the priming powder in the pan. As the pyrites falls against the spinning wheel the sparks set off the charge. (9) English snaphance pistol, dated 1593. A flint attached to the jaws of a cock is forced back against a spring and swung down when the trigger releases the spring. The flint strikes the face of a steel mounted on a pivoted arm above the pan of priming powder, producing sparks in much the same way as striking a flint to light a fire. Some snaphances were fitted with manual pan covers, others were opened automatically as on wheellocks. (10) Powder flask; a carrying cord passed through the pierced lug each side.

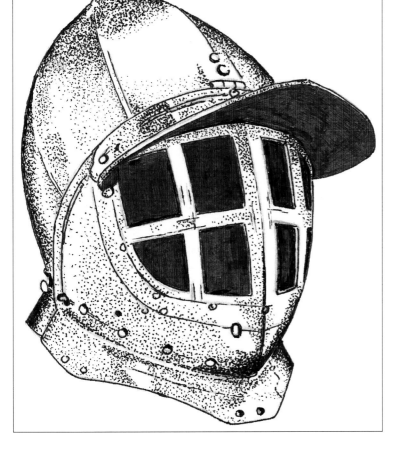

LEFT **Greenwich burgonet with octagonal skull, c.1590, with a barred face-guard hinged at the brow. (Author's collection)**

INDEX

References in **bold** refer to illustrations